How to Become A
GOOD MANAGER

Dr Aparna Chattopadhyay

Published by

F-2/16, Ansari Road, Daryaganj, New Delhi-110002
☎ 011-23240026, 011-23240027 • *Fax:* 011-23240028
Email: info@vspublishers.com • *Website:* www.vspublishers.com

Regional Office : Hyderabad
5-1-707/1, Brij Bhawan (Beside Central Bank of India Lane)
Bank Street, Koti, Hyderabad - 500 095
☎ 040-24737290
E-mail: vspublishershyd@gmail.com

Branch Office : Mumbai
Jaywant Industrial Estate, 2nd Floor–222, Tardeo Road
Opposite Sobo Central Mall, Mumbai – 400 034
☎ 022-23510736
E-mail: vspublishersmum@gmail.com

Follow us on

All books available at www.vspublishers.com

© Copyright: *V&S Publishers*
Edition 2017

The Copyright of this book, as well as all matter contained herein (including illustrations) rests with the Publisher. No person shall copy the name of the book, its title design, matter and illustrations in any form and in any language, totally or partially or in any form. Anybody doing so shall face legal action and will be responsible for damages.

Printed at : Repro Knowledgecast Limited, Thane

Author's Note

In today's organizations, the dramatic changes in technology, the international arena and workplace demographics, have all greatly affected continual challenges. Changes in organizational structures resulting from mergers, consolidations, and expansion have become the rule, rather than the exception.

The change in the global economy is affecting every individual and altering the management landscape and job opportunities. We face today a world of turbulence and uncertainty, where we can no longer count on a stable world that is unchanging and unvarying. Change is the only constant. It demands changes in ourselves, our approaches, our skills, our attitudes and our strategies.

All this necessitates developing 'people's skills' which requires understanding why people behave as they do. Such a knowledge significantly enhances personal effectiveness of employer in any organization.

This book caters to the for enhancing HR and OB (Human Resource and Organizational Behaviour). It aims at motivating people in organizational settings for developing teamwork and creating conducive work climates. It's emphasis is on people rather than money, materials and machines, while working towards the attainment of goals.

It aims at developing skills to meet the new challenges in the present day work scenario. It presents fundamental behavioural science concepts and simple-to-use psychological tips for attaining success in the career arena. As this requires the knowledge and application of tested behavioural science concepts plus the "timing" skills to get things done, this book will help you not only to acquire the basic knowledge but also to develop the attitudinal and emotional skills necessary to be a high performing leader. It focuses on (a) attitudinal changes, (b) knowledge changes, (c) individual behavioural changes and (d) group or organizational behavioural changes. It presumes that changes in knowledge lead to human skills followed by changes in attitude, which ultimately lead us to our coveted road to success.

No matter where you are, who you are, what you have accomplished, when or where or why you may not have realized your dreams—here is an opportunity for you to make a success of your career. Apply these principles of psychological research to your day-to-day work life and colonize your success.

—**Aparna Chattopadhyay**

Contents

Are You A Change Leader?... 7
Are You A Good Manager?... 10
Are You A Transparent Groupleader?... 12
Are You A Conformist or A Change-maker?... 15
Are You An ACE Knowledge Manager?... 18
Are You An Achiever in Your Organisation?... 20
Are you Rational in your Thoughts and Behaviour?... 22
Assess Your Time Management Profile... 24
Your Attitudes at Work... 29
Can You Counteract Strain?... 32
Can You Effectively Manage
Conflicts in Your Organisation?... 35
Can You Interact Successfully with
Different Personality Types?... 39
Can You Interact Successfully in
Cross-cultural Organisations?... 45
Do You Foster Team Development in Your Organisation?... 49
The Workers' Wants... 52
Do You Like Your Job?... 56
Are You Gender-friendly at Work... 59
How Creative Are You?... 62
How Well Do You Interact Within Your Workgroup?... 66
Can You Get to Open-up Others?... 71
Are You A Good Listener?... 73
The Self-actualization Approach... 76

Success or Failure at Work	79
Take A Peep into Your Value Orientation	82
Get An Aura	86
What is Your Organization Type?	90
On Your Own	94
Your Life-style Influences Your Work Output	97
Do You have the Potential to Re-invent Yourself?	102
Your Personality – Occupational Type	104
Your Work Psychology	107
Are You a Victim of the Achievement Trap?	110
Are You a Winner?	115
Are You People-centred?	118
Do You Work with Scientific Spirituality in Your Work Environment?	122
Your Knowledge Quotient of Multi-cultural Issues	125

■■■

Are You A Change Leader?

Interestingly, the only thing that is constant and that we can depend on is the inevitable occurrence of change. Consequently, dramatic economic and technological changes taking place in our organizations during the past few decades have resulted in causing a real challenge for the HRD professionals. It has necessitated not only finding and hiring employees who have basic business skills, but also on-going job training for managers and employees. New technologies require job re-training and motivational training. Consequently organizations have to spend huge amounts on training. Mc Elwain (1991) suggests that as much as fifty million of the workers currently employed in the US are in need of additional training to develop them on personal and professional levels and to enhance their attitude to work. As a result, many organizations are dedicating larger percentages of their budgets to personnel procurement and development for selecting and training employees to deal with the complexities of the changing technological scenario of today.

Change is inevitable and impermanent. It is inherently neither good nor bad. Most people perceive change as disruptive and to be avoided whenever possible. The key is to recognize that change is neutral, i.e., it occurs, and that it is perceived as good or bad depending on the conditions.

To manage change successfully one must stay flexible and be able to respond to what is going on. The more the change is described as what is presently happening—rather than what should be happening or what might happen next—the easier it will be to work with people in facilitating the change. The change leader's most important function is helping people to understand that they have the skills needed to implement positive change and are already using them effectively in their lives both at work and at home.

Every changed leader has a unique and distinct style from autocratic, participative and supportive to laissez- faire types. These styles of change leadership are intended to manage change.

Answering the following quiz shall enable you to determine the extent to which you are a change leader. **Answer the queries with a True or False answer in case you agree or disagree with them:**

1. Change is best facilitated by developing ownership in the change process.
2. Change leadership involves helping people to make better choices in light of current realities and then assisting them in taking full responsibility for making these choices happen.
3. Power is the ability to get what you want, resistance is the ability to avoid what you do not want. Resistance is thus a subset of power, not of change.
4. People can best work with resistance to change from others by first understanding and accepting their own.
5. Resistance to change is best dealt with by honouring it, rather than suppressing, avoiding, or minimizing it.
6. People do not resist change; they resist pain or the threat of it.
7. In order to bring about change, the change leader should make demand and the group is expected to respond without any negotiations.
8. A change leader should himself be involved with the change and negotiate the change with the group.
9. The change leader should not be directly involved in making the change happen. He should focus on how the group is working and make sure that everyone has a chance to speak his views and that the conflict issues are handled together reasonably.
10. The change leader should create the change and/or implement and then disengage himself from the group.
11. The vision of change leaders' employees must precede that of their organization.
12. It is imperative that before hoping to change one's employees

the change leader must change himself first.

Scoring

Assign one mark for every **'True'** response.

Interpretation

9-12: You are an excellent change leader who follows a productive change process and understands the dynamics of organizational change and its phases and intricacies. You are apt at presenting the change as well as working with the resistance productively.

5-8: You are a fairly balanced change leader and tackle the change situations quite smoothly in your organization.

1-4: You seem to lack an understanding of the basics of change dynamics. You must remember that the role of the change leader is to provide a process that will facilitate a specific change easily and effectively with minimum disruption and maximum support from the group. You can even initiate or implement change through a group member and not necessarily by yourself. You need to be more pro-active. If changes are planned and implemented effectively and if they are supported by appropriate training, the results may be measured in terms of greater productivity, higher morale, increased quality and reduced costs.

■ ■ ■

Are You A Good Manager?

Human resource development and people empowerment have gained increased attention in the recent years and are considered vital for the success of any organisation. Most often environmental conditions and conditions of work contribute to the empowerment or disempowerment as well as loss of skill and motivation of employees. Managers of organizations have thus to devote undivided attention to develop appropriate conditions at their workplace for energising as well as empowering their employees.

Relevant research in this sphere suggests analysis of conditions leading to employees' sense of powerlessness; implementation of suitable managerial strategies such as information sharing and providing autonomy to employees for enhancing their self-efficacy, creativity and initiative. Organizational factors such as bureaucratic work culture, dominative supervisory styles, inadequate reward system and job design, lack of autonomy and influence, etc. have been significantly correlated to the powerlessness and disillusionment of the employees.

Organisational research further reveals that income and amenities like housing, proper sanitation, drinking water and canteen facilities, medical care, amenities for women, environmental safety etc. have emerged as very significant predictors of life-satisfaction as well. Such objective conditions are also found to be highly correlated to satisfaction, trust and support, supervisory behaviour and peer relations and nature of job at the workplace.

Often managers with high need for dominative/authoritarian influence tend to create interpersonally aggressive and competitive work climate in the organization which creates hostility in the organization instead of promoting team work, participation and cooperation.

Take the following quiz and assess your own dominative vs integrative leadership style as a manager.

As a manager do you make a conscious effort to provide the following opportunities to your employees:—

1. Opportunity to learn something new, for example, skill and management, technical work, new jobs etc.
2. Fringe benefits to employees such as education of their children, medical facilities for their families etc.
3. Good salary scales.
4. Happy relationships between subordinates and supervisors.
5. Adequate drinking water and canteen facilities.
6. Feedback and genuine appreciation of their good work.
7. Respecting their views and suggestions.
8. Providing a good variety to them in their job roles.
9. Good scope for their skills and abilities to be used in their jobs.
10. Good recreation facilities.
11. Good influence over decisions pertaining to their own welfare and interest.
12. Freedom in doing their jobs without interference from their supervisors.
13. Recognition with regard to their aptitude to do their jobs well.
14. Providing them up-to-date information about events in the organisation

Scoring

Assign one mark for every **'yes'** answer.

Interpretation

10-14: Integrative and democratic leadership style.

5-9: Fairly enabling orientation.

0-4: Dominative leadership style.

■ ■ ■

Are You A Transparent Groupleader?

Research indicates that leader's self-disclosure or 'transparency' is correlated with productivity, creativity and personal growth of his group. The theory of Trust, Openness, Realization and Interdependence (TORI) has been applied to group and team training in industrial, educational and religious systems which revealed that when the trust level is high, the behaviour of the members of the group is more personal, more open, more self - determining, and more independent. When the trust level is low, members' behaviour becomes more impersonal, closed, 'ought' - determined, and more dependent and counter dependent. A study conducted by Dies &Cohen(American Psychologists at Maryland) further revealed that members indicated a preference for a leader who is confident in his or her leadership abilities and emotional stability and who is willing to share positive strivings(personal and professional goals) and normal emotional experiences such as worries and anxieties and feelings of pride, loneliness, sadness, helplessness, and anger.

On the other hand, members expressed reservations about the appropriateness of a group leader confronting individual members, especially early in the group sessions, with such negative feelings such as distrust, anger, prejudice, and disdain, or offering criticism of the overall group experience by admitting feelings of frustration, boredom, or isolation.

The quiz below represents a range of topics that leaders of organizations may share with their group members. The statements are constituted to include external past and present issues and here - and - now attitudes,feelings of the leader towards himself or herself, group members or the group as a whole.

You are to indicate how helpful or harmful you feel it would be for you to share each statement within the context of your group interactions. Before every item write the number on helpful to harmful continuum ranging from 1–7 that best represents your feelings about the appropriateness of that self disclosure or personal revelation. The continuum would reveal your feelings as: 7; Very helpful, 6; Helpful, 5; Somewhat Helpful, 4; Neutral, 3; Somewhat Harmful, 2; Harmful, 1; Very Harmful.

Respond according to your own beliefs, rather than the way you think others might respond. Also respond as if each disclosure is true of you.

Statements
Topics I might share with my group:
1. Guilt feelings of my psyche if any.
2. Whether or not I ever cry as an adult when I am sad.
3. The greatest point of disagreement I have(or have had) with my parents.
4. One of the worst things that ever happened to me.
5. Times I almost had, or did have, trouble with the law.
6. Times when I have felt helpless.
7. Times when I have not been dependable.
8. Times when I have been discouraged in my work.
9. Past experiences of failure as a group leader.
10. Times I have 'played sick' or wanted to get out of something.
11. Whether or not I am able to let myself go when I get angry.
12. My professional goals.
13. How I feel my colleagues view me, i.e. how they assess my competence.
14. My feelings about how much independence I need.
15. The aspects of my personality that I dislike, worry about, or regard as a handicap.
16. Feelings I have when I am severely criticized.
17. Questions about my emotional stability.
18. The admission that I have many conflicts that are similar to those of my group members.
19. Feelings of anxiety or uncertainty about my leadership.
20. What feelings, if any, I have trouble expressing or controlling.
21. Feelings of fondness toward another member in the group.
22. My feeling of isolation from the group.
23. My disgust toward a group member.

24. Times I almost had, or did have a clash with my group.
25. My worry about acceptance by the group members.
26. My protective feelings towards specific group member(s).
27. The fear that group will fail.
28. The worry that I am less sensitive than some of the group members.
29. My feelings of being inferior to other members in the group.
30. My feelings that what the members are doing is ridiculous.

Scoring

Items no. 1-10 deal with disclosing your personal history as a group leader. Sum your ratings to these items and divide by 10 to obtain your average helpfulness rating in this area. Write your average score here:

Items no. 11-20 focus on your personal characteristics and on your disclosure of present personal characteristics. Sum these ratings and divide by 10, and write your average score here:

Items no. 21-30 contain your reactions to what is occurring in the group and to individual members - i.e. your Here - and - Now reactions. Sum your ratings for those ten items and compute your average here:

Interpretation

Locate your averages by writing as "X" on each of the three continuums below and compare your beliefs about what is helpful for you as the group leader to disclose within group meetings.

Personal History	Very Helpful	Neutral	Very Harmful
	7 6 5 4 3 2 1		
Personal Characteristics	Very Helpful	Neutral	Very Harmful
	7 6 5 4 3 2 1		
Here–and–Now Reactions	Very Helpful	Neutral	Very Harmful
	7 6 5 4 3 2 1		

Are You A Conformist or A Change-maker?

Linda Moore, in her book titled *Release from Powerlessness: a Guide for taking Charge of Your Life* (1991) uses the intriguing metaphor "colouring between the lines" to express a conformist's behavior of doing just what one is told. In a *Peanut* cartoon, impressed with Sally's All-A report card, Charlie Brown asks her how she managed it. She explains that she is a good student who is not tardy and does what she is told. "And", she adds, "I colour between the lines!"

Interestingly, the reasons Sally offers for her perfect report card are all behavioral. She has clearly learned an important lesson: Behaviour can count as much —or even more than—substantive performance. Unfortunately the behaviour that gets her a good report card today—particularly doing just what she is told and colouring between the lines—can one day lead her to unproductive and self-defeating results, the pattern that we call conformity or co-dependence. Such a pattern results in a restricting and confining behavioral repertoire. It sets limits. It narrows vision and cramps one's style. It does not allow one the freedom to do anything but colour perfectly between the already drawn lines. It creates problems in the workplace. In certain types of mechanical jobs such as book-keeping, airplane engine maintenance, etc requiring following pre-set patterns meticulously, or when problems are few and solutions are straight-forward within a stable environment, colouring-between-the-lines approach generally works well.

But it is when initiative, creativity and flexibility are required, that the limitation imposed by conformity and co-dependence become more than obvious. The co-dependence bug traps organizations, as well as individuals inside narrow boundaries, suffocating imagination and inhibiting the development and adoption of novel situations or initiatives. It interferes with people's abilities to manage conflict, communicate and share information, build and maintain relationships and work smart.

Today's challenging and rapidly changing world is unlikely to grant us our wish to work in a stable environment and the demands of the changing work environments provide less and less possibility for accommodating co-dependent or conforming individuals.

Answer the following quiz to find out which type befits you.

1. Do you find it too hard to please others, particularly the authority figures?

    Yes/No

2. Do you become an overdemanding perfectionist or an over-responsible martyr, or a workaholic in order to avoid meaningful relationships?

    Yes/No

3. Can you deal with your differences by sharing your feelings about these differences with your co-workers?

    Yes/No

4. Are you capable of direct and open communication within your organization?

    Yes/No

5. Are you willing to say 'no' to avoid bad news?

    Yes/No

6. Has your co-dependent behaviour as a manager resulted in consequences such as alienation, anomie, manipulations, hidden agendas, broken promises and lies in your organisation?

    Yes/No

7. Do you find yourself to be rather a square peg in a round hole, in the changing nature of customer service which demands a new breed of worker—one who is empathetic, flexible, inventive, and able to work with minimal levels of supervision?

    Yes/No

8. Do you possess the skills and behavioral patterns for working smart—i.e. focussing your time, energy, and resources on the tasks at hand, setting priorities, putting the human as well the material and financial resources of the organization to good use?

9. Do you require well-defined boundaries and become anxious in the face of change?

Yes/No

10. Do you strongly resent changes in office design such as working in a cluster of open offices, to encourage impromptu meetings and more spontaneous informal communication between the chief executives and their co-workers?

Yes/No

11. Do you often portray yourself as a creatively abrasive person, sharp, scratchy, harsh and almost unpleasant individual who sees and tells others about things as they really are?

Yes/No

12. Can you deliver bad news constructively to others?

Yes/No

13. Which of the two approaches would you opt for your organization: a) colouring-between-the-lines approach and b) initiative, personal responsibility and flexibility?

Yes/No

14. Which one would you prefer to use for your writing purposes: a) ruled paper or b) unruled paper?

Yes/No

Scoring

Assign one mark for every **Correct** Answer.

Correct Answer

Question numbers 1, ,2 ,5, 6, 7, 9, 10, 13 a) and 14 a) have 'No' answers.

Question numbers 3, 4, 8, 11, 12, 13 b) and 14 b) have 'Yes' answers.

Interpretation

9-14: Highly individualistic.   **5-8:** Fairly conformist

1-4: Highly conformist

■ ■ ■

Are You An ACE Knowledge Manager?

In the current Internet era most of our organizations are passing through a transition phase resulting to a substantial communication stress on employees at different levels. The changing trends reveal that successful organizations tend to emphasize on providing a competitive-cum-innovative work environment for their employees.

As the level of specialization is escalating fast in organizations, a need for newer communication and information technology is simultaneously rising which needs to be assimilated by the employees in organizations. In the words of Hopburn, the well-known sociologist, this phenomenon refers to the 'cultural lag' denoting a distinct gap between the cultural change and the technological change. To bridge this gap, organizations require today a specialized manpower who can mobilize and direct employees to assimilate the new information technology and offer knowledge-based solutions leading to a higher level of efficiency. A typical profile of such a Chief Knowledge Officer (CKO) is unique in the sense that on one hand he requires a thorough understanding of the work environment, work ethics, and work attitudes of the employees of his organisation, and on the other, he looks forward to a constant search, validation and processing of the latest information technology developed globally. His constant concern and strategies have to encourage and foster these so that they are conducive to each other in reducing the cultural lag.

If you aspire to be one of these prestigious CKOs, think over and assess yourself on the following quiz:

1. Are you ready to take the initiative to gather the latest developments in Information Technology (IT) and allied areas which may contribute to your organizational efficacy?

2. Are you entrepreneurial enough to adopt a new project in your organization by involving successful experiences from other quarters?
3. Do you keep yourself abreast with the latest communication and information technology through the Internet and other sources?
4. Do you, on regular basis, share the new ideas and new technologies with your co-workers for improving their efficacy?
5. Do you have a nose for new events, new phenomena happening around you and your organizaion locally, nationally, and globally?
6. Are you able to foresee the extent to which a project could be implemented in the light of available software and hardware resources in your organization?
7. Do you enjoy working in a group project which aims at fostering team effort and team spirit?
8. Are you flexible in decision-making in case of any unforeseen changes within your organization?
9. Do you encourage your subordinates and co-workers to work on new technology, both hardware and software?
10. Do you as a manager, like to link up the career development/ special incentive with the level of IT usage in your organisation?

Scoring

Assign one mark for every **'yes'** answer.

Interpretation

7-10 : Basically you are an organization man who is committed and has a very clear sense of purpose. You have a quest for new knowledge acquisition of IT and using it meaningfully across your organization. Keep it up.

4-6 : You have a fair level of exposition and implementation of new technology in your work environment and need to work harder to achieve a still higher level of application of IT in your work environment.

1-3 : You have a long way to go. You require redefining your attitude so that you acquire and share new information technology with your co-workers more meaningfully. For this you have to create a conducive environment in your organization for a search for new knowledge and sharing the same with your colleagues.

■ ■ ■

Are You An Achiever in Your Organisation?

Psychological research has revealed that motivation is a key topic in work psychology. The answer to queries such as; "How can I get my people to work harder?" often lies in awareness about their motivational levels. A motive force is a person's reason for doing something. It is thus concerned with factors which push one or pull one to behave in certain ways. This in turn, has direct bearing on the need-based approach to motivation. Need for achievement or self-actualisation concerns the desire to overcome obstacles, to exercise power and to strive to do something difficult, and to the best of one's ability. This formed the basis of the theory of work motivation (Mc. Clelland, 1961), which states that enhancing the population's need for achievement is essential for a country's economic prosperity. Self-actualisation, which was regarded by Maslow as the pinnacle of human and organisational growth, can be identified on certain dimensions, as only a few of us tend to operate at that level.

Examine the following quiz to see whether you do, and whether Maslow's description of a fully functioning person matches yours.

Do you:

1. *Perceive people and events accurately,* without undue interference from your own preconceptions?
2. *Accept self and others,* including imperfections but seek improvement where possible?
3. *Tend to be spontaneous,* especially in your thoughts and feelings?
4. *Focus on problems outside self,* rather than being insecure and introspective?
5. *Tend to be autonomous,* and remain true to self despite pressure to conform?

6. *Tend to be detached,* so that you are not unduely thrown off course by awkward events?
7. *Appreciate good and beautiful things,* even if they are familiar?
8. *Have peak experiences* of intense positive emotions of a sometimes mystic quality?
9. *Have close relationships,* but only with a few carefully chosen people?
10. *Respect others,* avoid making fun of people and evaluate them according to their inner qualities rather than race or social class?
11. *Have firm moral standards,* and sense of right or wrong, though these may be different from many other people?
12. *Tend to be creative,* i.e. are open-minded and open to your experience, seeing things in novel ways and can draw novel conclusions from established information?

Scoring

Assign one mark for every **'yes'** answer.

Interpretation

9-12: The motivation to achieve, based on the belief that performance is "good" in itself forms your work ethics. You have a preference for challenging tasks and follow the pursuit of excellence i.e. a desire to perform to the best of your ability. You are agile and vibrant, aspiring for climbing the status hierarchy through healthy competition with your fellow beings and colleagues. You possess leadership qualities in your work approach.

5-8: You are sufficiently motivated and open to your experience. You are self confident and familiar with the means to accomplish your goals. You try to choose moderately difficult but realistic tasks so as to ascertain success in your work.

1-4: You seem to be stuck with the tyranny of your inner blocking—avioding an all-out effort or a true test of your ability. Your self-defeating emotional climate hinders your achievement level. Better introspect for a while and set realistic goals for achievement. A sense of achievement shall play a great role in changing your style of thinking.

Are you Rational in your Thoughts and Behaviour?

Psychologists such as Maslow, hold that some people tend to reach a healthier, more optimal level of functioning than the average person. Such people are relatively free from major psychological problems and have made the best possible use of their talents and strengths. Compared to the average person, these people have certain characteristics in common, such as continued freshness of appreciation of everyday realities; greater acceptance of themselves and others, high creativity and high resistance to conformity. By and large our inner core of growth need to be relatively weak and undeveloped, making it hard to discover and be easily stifled by disturbing circumstances. All things considered, personal development tends to be a struggle between growth-fostering and growth-discouraging forces.

To assess your own level of psychological growth and rational thinking, indicate your agreement or disagreement with each of the following statements by placing the appropriate number in the blanks before each item. Assign your scores as follows— 1 = disagree, 2 = somewhat disagree, 3 = somewhat agree, 4 = agree.

1. I do not feel ashamed of any of my emotions.
2. I feel I must do what others expect me to do.
3. I believe that people are essentially good and can be trusted.
4. I fail to be angry at those I love.
5. It is always necessary that others approve of what I do.
6. I don't accept my own weaknesses.
7. I can like people without having to approve of them.
8. I fear failure.
9. I avoid attempts to analyze and simplify complex domains.
10. It is better to be yourself than to be popular.

11. I have no mission in life to which I feel especially dedicated.
12. I can express my feelings even when they might result in undesirable consequences.
13. I do not feel responsible to help anybody.
14. I am bothered by fears of being inadequate.
15. I am loved because I give love.

Scoring

To get your score, responses placed before items 2, 4, 5, 6, 8, 9, 11, 13, 14 should be reversed (4=1, 3=2, 2=3, 1=4). Then add the resulting numbers to the responses of the rest of the items. Your total score can range between 15-60.

Interpretation

High score (50 and above)

You tend to live in the present rather than in the past; with guilt and regret; or in the future, with overidealized goals and fears. You also tend to be inner-directed, extraverted, and rational in your thoughts and behaviours.

Average score (31-49)

You have a fair ability for perceiving and experiencing yourself in relation to your environment. You realize that you begin to live authentically only as you affirm your inherent human freedom and take responsibility for your lives. You are aware that self-actualization is more of a life-long process that enhances the meaning of life rather than a readily attainable goal.

Below average score (15-30)

You must make conscious attempts to grow. Avoid attitudes that stunt your psyche. Such tendencies can cause neuroticism and maladjustment with your outside reality.

■ ■ ■

Assess Your Time Management Profile

It was a misty morning. I was sitting in a senior official's office at the transport department of NCT, as I had to collect my aunt's driving license papers. As I gazed at his messy desk in front of me, overflowing with papers, I wondered as to how on earth one could fish out an important document out of that sea of overflowing papers! And yet, to my amazement, the officer did not take much time to hand over to me the particular documents I needed. I realised that though he seemed to be utterly disorganised, he was, in fact, organised in his own manner.

More often than not, each one of us has a unique style of organising our work and managing our time. Some people are naturally quite organised; others are not. Some are even afraid that being too organised might stunt their creativity and spontaneity. Others feel comfortable with a structured organisational system. Some workers are good at doing many things at once, some are easily distracted by outside influences. By understanding your own strengths and areas of improvement in time-management as related to your work, you can focus your attention on the dimensions of time-management that are most problematic to you—as well as discover your own unique approach to time-management.

Your personality in terms of managing time and priorities can be described according to five different dimensions:1) attention to task, 2) type of focus, 3) approach to structure, 4) style of processing and 5) strategy of action. When you understand how best you function in terms of time management, you can develop organisational systems that work best for you.

The following quiz aims at giving you an insight into this:

How often is each of the following statements true for you? Write your answer on the blank before each item, using the following scale:

    4 = Almost always
    3 = Often
    2 = Sometimes
    1 = Almost never

1. I often get distracted by the unimportant while I am in the middle of the important. _____
2. My mind wanders when I am working alone. _____
3. Interruptions throughout the day affect the amount of work I am able to accomplish. _____
4. I put off today what I can do tomorrow. _____
5. If a party is being planned, I enjoy attending to the particulars more than to the theme. _____
6. I go home with my desk in order. _____
7. It is important to capture specific details of business conversation and record them verbatim. _____
8. I enjoy implementing the details of a project more than I do envisioning the end result. _____
9. I find myself losing sight of long-term goals when dealing with short-term crisis. _____
10. I put off making decisions until a situation becomes urgent. _____
11. I prepare for things at the last minute. _____
12. I find myself working long hours and never catching up. _____
13. I know where I have filed most of my papers. _____
14. I keep my "to-do" list handy. _____
15. Telephone and fax numbers for my business contacts are readily accessible. _____
16. I object to meetings that start late. _____
17. I tend to take on several tasks at one time. _____
18. While working on one project, ideas about other projects come to my mind. _____
19. I am eager to start a new project before I finish an existing project. _____

20. During a business phone conversation, I would rather look for a related file while talking than put the person on hold. _____

Scoring

For scoring of your statements, club your scores under the following sections:

Section 1: Attention to task

1. _____
2. _____
3. _____
4. _____
Total _____

Section 2: Type of focus

5. _____
6. _____
7. _____
8. _____
Total _____

Section 3: Strategy of action

9. _____
10. _____
11. _____
12. _____
Total _____

Section 4: Approach to structure

13. _____
14. _____
15. _____
16. _____
Total _____

Section 5: Style of processing

17. _____
18. _____

19. _____
20. _____

Interpretation

Adding up the total score for each section separately will give you the following profile of your time-management style. Check your scores.

Section 1: Attention to task

7 and above: You have a "divergent" attention to task. Though your desk may be messy, you would maintain that you know exactly where everything is. You tend to easily wander off the subject to whatever sounds interesting at the moment. You draw energy from starting new projects but are not very particular in finishing them.

1-6: Your attention to task is that of the "convergent" type of category. You draw energy from completing projects and targets. Working with divergent people can be a challenge for you.

Section 2: Type of focussing

7 and above: You are a detail-oriented person who needs facts and details about a situation in order to feel comfortable. You seek out information and verification and prefer situations that can be supported by facts and figures. You draw energy from seeking and organising information.

1-6: You belong to the globally oriented type of personality who is more drawn to "possibilities" than the facts of current reality. You enjoy thinking about the future and discussing interrelationships. You often have highly tuned conceptual skills and are drawn to professions such as theatre, the arts, upper management and marketing. Although some globally oriented people also enjoy taking care of the subsequent details, most do not.

Section 3: Strategy of action

7 and above: You tend to be a "reactive" individual who likes putting off today what can be done tomorrow and as a result, spend a lot of your time responding to crises or deadlines that pop up suddenly.

1-6: You belong to the "proactive" category of individuals who take charge of their day and accomplish what they set out to accomplish. You often do not let circumstances or procrastination get in your way. Once you make a plan, you follow it and consequently rarely find yourself in last-minute crisis situations.

Section 4: Approach to structure

7 and above: You believe in having a loose approach to structure and prefer to have flexibility in how you carry out tasks. You are fine with meetings starting late and even proceeding without an agenda. You put information wherever it is convenient at the time, resulting in many scraps of paper with valuable information scattered on your desk. You put together some system of working in the beginning, but as the project proceeds, you alter the system or ignore it completely.

1-6: You maintain a tight approach to structure and like to have a system for accomplishing tasks. You prefer that meetings start on time and follow a pre-designated agenda. You have specific places to put specific information. When working on a task, you will figure out how to organise and structure what you are going to do before you begin.

Section 5: Style of processing

7 and above: You are a parallel processor and are comfortable performing more than one task at a time. When you have to work with serial processors, you often feel frustrated at the seemingly slow pace of progress. You would rather keep all parts of a project in motion at the same time.

1-6: You are a serial processor and prefer to focus on the task at hand. In contrast to the parallel processors, you prefer to begin at the beginning and complete each step thoroughly before proceeding.

■ ■ ■

Your Attitudes at Work

Social psychologists maintain that attitudes, lasting beliefs about and the evaluations of specific aspects of the social or physical world, play an important role in shaping many aspects of the human psyche. They predict and regulate human behaviour. The *specific* attitudes held by an individual are more vital in behaviour shaping. The attitude you persistently hold affects your outlook towards life, and thus your behavior. "Two men look through the prison bars, one sees the mud, the other, the stars!"

Optimism and pessimism are thus a product of our attitude towards life and its multifarious facets. Psychotherapists aim at curing the mental disorders of the patients by bringing about a desirable change in their *attitudes* towards themselves and their problems. As they say, "We become what we think." Hence, our personalities are often shaped by our thoughts and attitudes.

Take a bird's eye view of your own attitudes, interests and behaviour from the following quiz and gain an understanding of the latent features of your inner self.

Selct the appropriate alternative from the following statements reflecting your behaviour and personality.

Are you the kind who:
Part 1.

1. Believe in planning ahead and feel
    a) Uneasy with last minute changes?
    b) Often change your mind at the last minute?
2. a) Organise things for your peer group, rather than advise them?
    b) Act as an adviser rather than as an organiser for the peer group?
3. a) Love to make presentations at meetings or social functions so as to be the centre of attention?

b) Like to work silently, away from the limelight?
4. a) Prepare a clear schedule of work before starting a task?
b) Prefer taking things as they come?
5. a) Prefer to plan meticulously so as to avoid the unexpected to the utmost?
b) Like to leave things unplanned and love the challenge of the unexpected?

Part 2.

6. a) Like to make decisions after analysing the situation thoroughly?
b) Depend on one's "gut feelings" for making decisions?
7. a) Find it relatively easier to befriend unknown people?
b) Require special effort to mix with unfamiliar people?
8. a) Follow a practical and down to earth approach to things in life?
b) Often dream of new ventures and ideas with one's "head-in-the-clouds?"
9. a) Are easy to get to know and like meeting lots of people?
b) Are the quiet types whose real self is not always known to others?
10. a) Generally listen to the dictates of their heads?
b) Usually let their hearts rule their heads?

Interpretation
Part 1.

Majority in A's : Organizer

A meticulous planner, you like to gather as much information as possible and put a lot of emphasis on working in an orderly manner. You do not like taking risks in life. "A place for everything and everything in its place seems to be your motto. You dislike slackness and ambiguity in life's events. You are endowed with tremendous energy and dynamism and a clear mental strength.

Majority in B's: Adventurer

Your love for the unstructured and ambiguous makes you an adventurer in spirit. You love to explore different possibilities even if it means delaying action. Your preference for complex problems makes you see possibilities in all problems. You come up with best ideas working by yourself and are fairly creative. You prefer to take life as it comes.

Part 2.

Majority of A's: Realist

You usually let your head rule your heart and are described by others as a "down to earth" individual. Your personal beliefs and feelings do not affect your decisions. You like to be convinced by fact rather than feelings. Outgoing and gregarious, you tend to see realities in all situations. You are too practical to be sensitive to the subtleties of life and like to reason out things to test their validity.

Majority of B's: Thinker

You prefer to work in depth on a few things at a time. Before doing a task you ask yourself "is it fair?" Your intuitive heart seems to rule all your decisions and solutions come clearer to you when you relate them to your sentiments. You like to go into the details of things and emphasize on getting ideas rather than facts. You tend to be highly imaginative and introvertish, prefering to mix only with a select few.

■ ■ ■

Can You Counteract Strain?

In the modern era of hectic, harrowing and fast pace, a great majority of our civilization experiences stress at some point or the other. Stress has become a major contributor, either directly or indirectly to coronary heart disease, cancer, lung ailments, accidental injuries, and cirrhosis of the liver and suicide. Stress seems to have become the price paid for becoming affluent and successful. Twice as many as high income as low-income people suffer from the tension of stress. Also, the more educated the people are, the more likely they are to suffer great stress.

Most often, stress consists largely of *how we* respond to events, not the events themselves, so that we bring a lot of stress on ourselves. Each of us reacts to stress, even the same stressor, somewhat differently. There are a number of ways in which we may attempt to alleviate stress spontaneously. Although these responses tend to occur automatically, they probably operate at a high level of awareness. Managing stress successfully involves much more than relying on the automatic, symptom reducing reactions to stress. It means taking charge, directing and controlling our responses to stressors, thereby modifying the overall stress, modifying one's environment and altering ourselves in one way are major techniques through which stress could be reduced to a major extent. Building up a greater tolerance for stress and changing your pace of life could be of tremendous help in this direction.

Well are *you* a well-adjusted person and adept at counteracting stress? Take the following quiz and discover your aptitude of stress management.

Do you often:

1. Get up early enough to avoid rushing?

2. Set an alarm to get ready at an early hour?
3. Take time for breakfast?
4. Make a list of things to do and put the most important things first?
5. Allow enough time to drive to school or work without rushing?
6. Walk at an unhurried pace?
7. Share at least one meal each day with other people?
8. Avoid the excess use of caffeine, alcohol or drugs?
9. Take some time out to relax each day such as going for a walk, riding your bike or taking a hot bath?
10. Avoid procrastination and believe that the sooner you begin a task, the lesser you'll worry about it?
11. Concentrate on the task at hand?
12. Take time to talk with your friends?
13. Set aside regular time for study?
14. Schedule some relaxation time aside on weekends to break the cycle of stress?
15. Jot down things you don't get done and you'd like to do the next day?
16. Unwind before going to bed such as reading a book or listening to music?
17. Control your distressful thoughts and take to creative visualization and meditation every day?

Scoring

Assign one mark for every **'yes'** answer.

Interpretation

11-17: You have the knack of managing stress rather successfully and enjoy better physical and mental health than the rest. Choosing to alter your lifestyle or modifying your environment intelligently, you succeed in combating the day to day stressful situations. You are wise enough to handle a stressful situation as a challenge, evoking the best in you for your personal growth.

6-10: You tend to take stress rather calmly in your stride. Your realistic attitude towards stress often enables you to deal with it quite well. You are not usually overcome by feelings of powerlessness even in very difficult situations. Your psychological hardiness empowers you to maintain a reasonable control of yourself and the stressful situations at hand, most of the times.

1-5: You are a sad victim of stress and feel highly strung most of the time. You find yourself unable to concentrate, preoccupied by worries and feel you are losing out on things. Once you get a personal grip on stress, you can deal with it more effectively. For example, if you are the physical type, you might choose one of the relaxers: aerobics, biking, swimming, walking, progressive relaxation or soaking in a hot bath or sauna. However if you're more of a cerebral type, you might try one of these relaxers: meditation, writing, reading, crossword puzzle, television, listening to relaxing music, painting, chess or card games. In most cases, you may choose a combination of ways to unwind. The important thing, however, is to find what works best for you.

■ ■ ■

Can You Effectively Manage Conflicts in Your Organisation?

Conflicts are inevitable in organisations owing to different personality styles and job orientations of its group members. Conflicts, when explored and dealt with openly can enhance the organization, stimulating its work groups to creativity and create organisational commitment. Learning about the alternative means of handling conflict gives the manager a wider choice of actions to employ in any given situation.

As a manager, which one of the following strategies do you usually employ while managing conflicts in your organization?

1. When something bothers you in your organization, you tend to—
   a) Ignore the issue that bothers you to "get rid" of it.
   b) Need a cooling-off period with an agreed-on time to deal with the issue later.
   c) Work on the issue involved before the issue becomes intolerable to you.

2. If your organisation has a human resource professional on staff, you prefer to—
   a) Ignore him and act according to your own ability and potential to solve conflicts.
   b) Consult that professional for suggestions for how to approach the problem.
   c) Feel threatened by his expertise and surround yourself with your junior favourites.

3. If an individual often dances attendance upon you and takes to complaining about someone who is not present, do you—
   a) Believe him blindly and feel flattered by the attention he gives you?
   b) Treat the other person with prejudiced behaviour?
   c) Encourage him to talk directly with the other person and settle the conflict under your guidance or a human resource

professional?

4. If some group member of your organisation disagrees with you over an issue, do you—
   a) Regard that person as hostile and bad?
   b) Look for and feel more comforted with other group members who always agree with you?
   c) Remember that it is alright to disagree and that relationship is not destroyed but can be even enhanced by working towards a mutually satisfactory situation to a conflict?

5. While working on a conflict issue, how many of the following reminders do you give to yourself—
   a) Look for a "win/win" solution: an arrangement whereby both you and the other person involved "win."
   b) Do your best to put yourself in the other person's shoes.
   c) Be willing to "own" part of the problem as belonging to you (avoid "thinking that's not *my* problem")
   d) Remember that talking about your feelings is more effective than acting them out.
   e) Establish a common goal and stay focussed on it.
   f) At the end of the discussion with the other person, summarise what has been decided and who will take any next step.

6. While giving feedback to your employees, do you usually—
   a) *Describe* the other person's behaviour objectively by giving your *own* reaction to the behaviour?
   b) Use "judging" language?
   c) Use generalised terms such as adjectives and labels?

7. During interpersonal interaction with your group members, do you usually—
   a) Talk about what you want, considering your own needs of utmost priority?
   b) Listen to the other person's issue patiently, considering the needs of the other person as vital, who receives your feedback?
   c) Often dump feedback on your employees, even if it has not been requested?

8. When resolving conflicts, your overriding consideration is—
   a) Favouring your favourite flatterers only?
   b) Principles and organisational ideal and the larger good of the organisation?

c) Enhancing your personal ego and popularity by being in the good books of the majority of your employees?

9. In the competitive environment of your organisation, do you—
    a) Prefer to assign important and prestigious tasks only to a select few favourites of yours, thereby enhancing their promotion opportunities?
    b) Overload particular individuals of your organisation with routine and thankless jobs, which involve no incentives whatsoever?
    c) Employ methods to make your employees work together in a team and organise informal get-togethers for them?

10. A mistake by a subordinate of yours in a conflicting situation is treated by you as —
    a) Rejection of the person making the mistake.
    b) An experience from which lessons are to be learnt to prevent failure and improve performance in the future.
    c) A prejudiced behaviour towards the person who has committed the mistake.

Scoring

Assign one Mark for every **correct** answer.

Correct Answers:

1. c)
2. b)
3. c)
4. c)
5. **Assign one Mark for every reminder you give to yourself.**
6. a)
7. b)
8. b)
9. c)
10. b)

Maximum obtainable marks = 14

Interpretation

9-14: Congratulations! You are adept at preventing and solving managerial conflicts. You can manage work motivation of your employees by your open communication and due recognition to your subordinates. You believe in creating a climate of credibility and providing equal opportunities for the growth of your employees.

You promote positive reinforcement in a climate of empathy, trust and understanding of the needs of your staff.

5-8: You follow a fair approach towards your employees. In your interaction with your employees, you have the ability to resort to interpersonal conflicts fairly and objectively.

1-4: You have yet to learn the skills of effective human resource development and handling organisational conflicts. Conflict can be distributive and constructive. When mismanaged, conflict can destroy a group's effectiveness, when handled well, it can greatly increase the quality of a group's work and restore pride in its members. Train yourself to understand the dynamics of conflict management. In the first place, do not regard conflict as essentially negative in nature or something to be avoided. When well-managed, conflict is highly constructive, in fact it is essential to effective problem-solving discussions. Learn the constructive methods of dealing with it. You have to train your subordinates as to how to *disagree productively* in order to foster creativity, team spirit and commitment to group goals.

Handle unavoidable conflicts by -

a) *Systematic desensitization* : Perform relaxation techniques vividly imagining the impending conflict until you become tense and then resume the relaxation techniques. Repeat until the crisis has passed.

b) *Pushing down through relaxaton* : Condition yourself to relax when crises are imminent.

c) *Centering and self-monitoring* : Focus on the here and now during crisis rather than what may happen or has already happened and whether your body language expresses self-control.

d) *Putting it in perspective* : Believing that 'this too shall pass' can be liberating. Situations rarely turn out as badly as anticipated.

e) *Thought stopping or diversion* : By rationally blocking anxiety-producing thoughts, we can restore our emotional equilibrium.

■ ■ ■

Can You Interact Successfully with Different Personality Types?

We all spend a good part of our day interacting with our co-workers, our bosses, other departments, customers, suppliers and salespeople. Most of us are thus familiar with the principles and mechanics of interacting, but not really with the dynamics of negotiating differently with different types of living human beings. The five billion, or so, of us in the world are all unique. Yet we share traits that are similar to some, and different from others. That's why no two negotiations are ever alike. As a result, learning only one way to negotiate puts one at a disadvantage. It only works for people who fit that one specific mould—and they are very far between.

Personality Negotiating is a behavioural approach to interaction approach that enables you to use your natural communication and observation abilities to better understand others' negotiating styles. You do this by discovering and keying in on your personality traits and those of the people you're interacting with. Understanding how these personality traits influence behaviour lets you adapt your behavioural pattern with them. The personality theory in Personality Negotiating is based on Carl Jung's work on personality type. It is used in business today primarily as a management development tool. Thousands of companies, including Apple computers, ITT, and Digital Equipment Corporation administered the Myres—Briggs Type indicator (MBTI) (developed by psychologists Isabel Myres and Katherine Briggs) and other Jungian personality-type measures over two million times a year. This theory describes and categorizes behaviour four ways, with each category having two alternate preferences. The four categories are—

   a) Introvert/Extrovert
   b) Sensing/ Intuitive
   c) Thinking/Feeling

d) Judging/Perceiving

What's your type? To learn your personality type, and also of those with whom you interact, answer the following quiz, which will give you a good idea of your preferences. The quiz is based on the answers that people who have taken part in the MBTI gave in Sales and Negotiation Training Company's training seminars.

Also learn to use the distinctive strategies suited for each personality type, for successful interactions with them. Read each of these items and encircle answer A or B, depending on which response fits you the best. There are no right, wrong or better answers.

1. If someone asks you a question, do you usually:
   a) Reflect for a few moments, then respond?
   b) Respond quickly?

2. Do you like :
   a) Short meetings?
   b) Long meetings?

3. Would you rather go out with a few friends:
   a) To a quiet restaurant?
   b) To a crowded party?

4. Do you find your most tiring days to be:
   a) Days when you meet many new people?
   b) Days when you are alone?

5. Do you prefer:
   a) Introducing yourself to someone?
   b) Having someone introduce you?

6. If there is a long period of silence during a conversation, is it your inclination to:
   a) Fill it in?
   b) Use it to think?

7. When describing something, do you,
   a) Describe it literally?
   b) Describe it conceptually?

8. If someone gave you a proposal written on an inexpensive paper, would you,
   a) View that negatively?
   b) Probably not notice it or be bothered by it?

9. Do you tend to:
   a) Notice little things?
   b) Not notice little things?

10. Do you like buying things that are :
    a) The latest and the greatest?
    b) The tried and true?

11. When you make a decision, do you most want to know:
    a) How it fits into your future plans?
    b) How it benefits you immediately?

12. Are you swayed more by how:
    a) Concepts relate to facts?
    b) Facts relate to concepts?

13. If you're buying something for someone else, are you concerned:
    a) That you are buying the right thing?
    b) That they will like it?

14. When you think about several people with much in common, do you tend to think of them:
    a) As a group?
    b) As individuals?

15. Are your best buying decisions made:
    a) Rationally and precisely?
    b) Emotionally?

16. Do you like dealing with people who are:
    a) Nice?
    b) Predictable?

17. If you're in a negotiation and two people are arguing do you:
    a) Feel uncomfortable that there is disharmony?
    b) Assume that interpersonal conflict is unavoidable?

18. After trying with no luck to make disgruntled people happy, would you:
    a) Keep trying until you are successful?

b) Give up?

19. Do you tend to like days that are:
   a) Tightly scheduled?
   b) Spontaneous?

20. If you made a bad decision, would you feel:
   a) It was the best decision at the time?
   b) Like you were rushed?

21. If you're given a deadline for making a decision, and there is not enough time, would you:
   a) Make it anyway with the data you've got?
   b) Allow the deadline to slip until you have all the data?

22. If you came to a fork in the woods, would you take:
   a) The road less travelled?
   b) The road more travelled?

23. You have just made a big decision. Are you most likely to be:
   a) Worried it wasn't the right thing to buy?
   b) Relieved the decision was over?

24. When you buy something with several options, do you:
   a) Decide when you are comfortable that you have enough information?
   b) Set up a deadline for making a final decision, and then work to get all the information by that deadline?

Scoring

Introversion/ Extroversion scale
Add the a) answers for questions 1,2,3
Add the b) answers for questions 4,5,6
          Put the total here_____I/E

If the total score is 4 or more, you're most likely an **introvert**; otherwise you're most likely **an extrovert**.

Sensing/Intuitive scale
Add the a) answers for the questions 7,8,9
Add the b) answers for the questions 10, 11, 12
          Put the total here_____S/I

If the total score is 4 or more, you're most likely a **sensing** type; otherwise you're most likely an **intuitive** type.

Thinking/Feeling scale

Add the a) answers for questions 13, 14, 15
Add the b) answers for questions 16, 17, 18
    Put the total here_____ T/F

If the total score is 4 or more, you're most likely a **thinking** type; otherwise you're most likely a **feeling** type.

Judging/Perceiving scale

Add the a) answers for questions 19, 20, 21
Add the b) answers for questions 22, 23, 24
    Put the total here_____ J/P

If the total score is 4 or more, you're most likely a **judging** type; otherwise you're most likely a **perceiving** type.

How to Negotiate with Different Personality Types:

On the basis of these queries, determine the personality types of people with whom you interact. There can be several permutations and combinations of these basic personality types. Make use of the following strategies when negotiating with some of the personality types as under:

1. The Extrovert, Sensing, Thinking, Judging types (ESTJs):

Prepare well organised, neatly presented proposals rich in detail and documentation for them. Don't ever do guess work with them as this type of persons are very good at logical analysis of facts, and one wrong guess can lose their confidence. Present traditional, conservative solutions. New ideas need support from factual evidence.

2. The Extrovert, Sensing, Thinking, Perceiving types (ESTPs):

You can expect them to ask questions about facts but think to themselves "how logical is this?". Therefore, show them practical benefits of a proposal. If possible, provide prototype or model providing feasibility of solution.

3. Introverted, Sensing, Thinking, Perceiving types (ISTPs):

They are superior trouble-shooters. They make excellent spontaneous decisions and respond quickly and correctly in the midst of crisis. Some of the greatest generals were ISTPs. They have a dominant thinking function that's introverted. If your suggestion helps solve a crisis, it's likely to be a short negotiation. Send a copy of your ideas detailing immediate benefit. Present your information neatly and logically. Do not get too theoretical. They are put off by long, drawn out tedious negotiations. They get bored in non-crisis negotiations.

4. Introverted, Sensing, Thinking, Judging types (ISTJs):

As they have a dominant introverted sensing function and a secondary thinking function, they are sometimes averse to new ideas because of their traditional mindset and their inferior intuitive function. They are inclined to view anything untraditional very skeptically. They tend to think to themselves, "What are the missing details?" They dislike poorly organised and presented proposals and 'wild' ideas, especially those without factual support. They seldom make factual mistakes. Prepare highly detailed, well-supported, organised and neat proposals and send them before the meeting. This gives them time to go over the proposals privately and in-depth, so they will fully understand and appreciate your suggestions. Schedule meetings well in advance. Make sure that meetings don't run unnecessarily long.

The use of these personality negotiating styles shall focus on the strengths of your interactions, making you walk away a winner.

■ ■ ■

Can You Interact Successfully in Cross-cultural Organisations?

In today's world, multinational companies, world markets, advances in communications technology, and the reality of the 'global village' have created an environment that increasingly requires organisations to be inclusive, multi-cultural organisations. Thus in the present era we find an inevitable transition from a mono-cultural to culturally diverse, inclusive organisations around us. Achieving a successful, inclusive, multi-cultural organisation requires embracing and tapping diversity as a route to success. It requires new styles of leadership, thinking, communication, problem-solving, and strategic planning. It requires new organisational structures, practices, benefits, plans, behaviour patterns, values, goals—in short a complete systemic overhaul.

Ironically most people do not do really well when interacting in an organisational environment that is foreign to their own or with people having cultural preferences different from their own. This is particularly true within cross-cultural or cross-functional groups. Preferences regarding interpersonal interactions, group interactions and information may vary from one culture to another just as they also vary from one individual to another, regardless of cultural origin. People's interactive preferences need to be understood in order to facilitate productive group work.

Cross-cultural or cross-functional group settings can provide enriching opportunities to learn about ourselves through others as well as about others and their cultures. Things often take on new meanings in the context of other culture orientations.

Organisations have to develop realistic expectations about the challenges that lie ahead. For instance, an aggressive multi-cultural recruiting program would be counter-productive in an organisation whose culture, practices, and reward systems are exclusive and mono-cultural. Theorists have identified major dimensions of cultural variability such as 'context' comprising low context vs high context of people and cultures, socialization of information and people, spatial orientation, (monochronic vs polychronic individual orientations to time as used by Hall and Hall, 1990).

The following quiz (based on Maurice Graham and Dwight Miller's organisational development model at Brigham Young University, Hawaii) would enable you to identify your tendencies to interact in group activities of an organisation in which more than one cultural orientation is involved. The answers, however, will be useful only if you respond honestly. Respond to each item by filling in the blank what best describes your preference in terms of how strongly you agree or disagree with it using the following continuum:

SD = Strongly Disagree
D = Disagree
MD = Mildly Disagree
MA = Mildly Agree
A = Agree
SA = Strongly Agree

1. I work best when we share information and then reach consensus as a group.
2. Information should be held in common and not controlled by specific individuals or parts of the group.
3. It is best for all decisions to be approved by the whole group.
4. Experts within a group should be allowed to make decisions for the group.
5. Getting the details of needed information is more important than knowing who provided them.
6. I'm impatient when someone tries to explain something I already know.
7. I would trust the group members and support their shared interest even if I do not agree with them.
8. I would use the utmost diplomacy in order not to embarrass anyone while working through problems in the group.
9. Once a commitment has the group's approval, it is expected to be honoured.

10. I would decide on my own what should be done and how it should be done.
11. I would directly confront problems or conflicts between individuals in the group.
12. I would want understanding individual performers in group activities to be rewarded more than those who did not contribute as much.
13. I feel uncomfortable when there are individuals in the group who remain distant and don't interact with the group.
14. It is the best to have the leader in a centralized location where all members of the group can interact with him/her.
15. I don't like doing work on my own or being separate from the group.
16. I don't want to be interrupted when I'm working on or thinking about a problem.
17. I prefer to work alone until I'm ready to get with the group.
18. When working in a group, I prefer to work with individuals who think as I do.
19. I would desire lots of time and flexibility to accommodate the different personalities in the group.
20. It is important to take the time needed to develop or share ideas before making a decision than it is to meet deadlines.
21. Plans should always be open to change.
22. A group should not stop working or discussion until a solution is found or a decision is made.
23. The group should deal with only one thing at a time until a decision is made.
24. When the group has finished its work it is best to move on and form new relationships.

Interpretation

The statements denote the following dimensions of cultural variability:

1. Socialization of Information
Statements no. 1,2,3 denote high shared flow.
Statements no. 4,5,6 denote controlled flow.

2. Socialization of People
Statements no. 7,8,9 denote collectivist tendencies.

Statements no. 10, 11, 12 denote individualistic tendencies.

3. Spatial Orientation
Statements no. 13,14,15 denote shared tendencies.
Statements no. 16,17,18 denote personalised tendencies.

4. Time Orientation
Statements no. 19, 20, 21 denote polychronic tendencies.
Statements no. 22, 23, 24 denote monochronic tendencies.

Scoring

Questions 1, 2, 3, 7, 8, 9, 13, 14, 15, 19, 20, 21 have the following scoring key:
Strongly Disagree = 0
Disagree = 1
Mildly Disagree = 2
Mildly Agree = 3
Agree = 4
Strongly Agree = 5

Questions no. 4, 5, 6, 10, 11, 12, 16, 17, 18, 22, 23, 24 have the following scoring key:
Strongly Disagree = 5
Disagree = 4
Mildly Disagree = 3
Mildly Agree = 2
Agree = 1
Strongly Agree = 0

Interpretation

82-120: Higher ability to interact across cultural context.
41-81: Moderate ability to interact across-cultural context.
1-40: Lower ability to interact across cultural context.

■ ■ ■

Do You Foster Team Development in Your Organisation?

A healthy organisation is like a healthy individual. Its interpersonal competence cannot be enhanced unless individuals receive frank and accurate information regarding the impact of their behaviour upon others. Such knowledge provides the power to make those changes necessary to increase effectiveness in organizational behaviour. The values of a democratic society, in which participation, involvement, and responsibility are prized as desirable behaviours; are valuable not only to the individual in his pursuit of individual self-fulfillment and growth, but also to society in that they perpetuate and preserve the ideology of freedom of choice among a broadened range of alternatives and accountability for the choice to which one is committed.

In a team-building programme, members of functionally interdependent groups of an organisation are provided the opportunity to explore systematically the manner in which they relate to one another, the type of communication patterns they characterise in their group-interactions, the level of trust and openness that exists among them, their decision-making strategy within the organisation, the kind of influence that each one exerts upon the other and the level of satisfaction felt by each member with regard to such policy issues.

What is the level of team-building programme in your own organisation? Introspect and answer the following quiz to assess and analyze the deficiencies, if any, that carefully planned team-building strategies could remedy. Answer in a "Yes" or a "No".

Do you make conscious effort to see that in your organisation:
1. The employees are helpful to each other?
2. Any employee should be in a position to go to anybody else to discuss any problem he/she faces?
3. Employers and employees work together amicably with a team spirit?
4. Irrespective of the busy schedule and the workload, the employees find time to share their concerns with each other?
5. The employer and the employees trust one another?
6. Suggestions are often solicited from all levels of employees?
7. Employees receive credit and appreciation for finding out a different way of doing things, which nobody has ever done before?
8. Conscientious attempts are made to consider the values and views of employees concerned?
9. There is open and informal communication between the employer and the employees?
10. Relevant information is available and shared by all employees who need and use it for achieving high performance?
11. The employer has concern for his people, and communicates with them (including their criticism) out of such concern?
12. While taking decisions, special care is taken to maintain cordial relations with all concerned?
13. Listening to others with genuine interest encourages others to express themselves more freely and work together in a team?
14. Much of tension and anxiety is reduces by trusting fellow workers?
15. When changes are to be introduced, persons who will be affected by the change should be consulted?
16. Sometimes the best advice comes from the least of one's subordinates?
17. The team members treat others as they would like to be treated by others, for building team leadership?
18. The organisation is run on the principle that a co-operative decision leads to better implementation?
19. You must entrust responsibilities to your employees as human nature is fundamentally cooperative and needs recognition?
20. Creative permissiveness prevails in the organisation?

21. Every person in the organizational system perceives clearly that the other has also some power, and that he should not misuse his power by holding back information, delaying matters or giving misleading information to others?
22. Employees working together perceive the goals of their organisation as superordinate goals (shareable) and that each one realises that this cannot be achieved single-handedly but by working together harmoniously?
23. Group and individuals share certain norms and begin to see good points in each other so that collaboration prevails?
24. There is an organizational climate which is inspiring and free of favouritism?

Scoring

Assign one mark for every **'yes'** answer.

Interpretation

17-24: Excellent team spirit
9-16 : Moderate team spirit
1-8 : Poor team spirit.

■ ■ ■

The Workers' Wants

People in organisations have many needs, all of which are continually competing. No one person has exactly needs as another. Some people are drawn mainly by achievement, others are concerned primarily with security and so on. Despite these individual differences, an effective manager would not presume to decide which motives are important to his employees. If he has to understand, predict and control behaviour, he must know what his employees really want from their jobs. By bringing their perceptions closer and closer to reality, (i.e. what their people really want) managers can increase their effectiveness.

What Do Workers Want?

For decades, research has been conducted among employees in the U.S. industry in an attempt to answer the question: "What do workers want?" In one such study (conducted in U.S. in 1949) supervisors were asked to try *to put themselves in a worker's shoes* by ranking in order of importance a series of items that workers may want from their jobs. In addition to the supervisors, the workers themselves were asked to rank these same items in terms of what they wanted most from their jobs. The results showed the following interesting ranks on the items:

As is evident from the results, the supervisors in this study generally ranked good wages, job security, promotion and good working conditions as the things workers want most from their jobs. On the other hand, workers felt that what they wanted most was full appreciation for work done, feeling "in" on things, and sympathetic understanding of personal problems—all incentives that seem to be related to affiliation and recognition motives. Only job security was among the top four concerns of both workers and supervisors, but the former ranked it fourth whereas the latter ranked it second. The other top three things that workers indicated

Items	Supervisors	Workers
Good working conditions	4	9
Feeling "in" on things	10	2
Tactful disciplining	7	10
Full appreciation for work	8	1
Management's loyalty to workers	6	8
Good wages	1	5
Promotion and growth with the company	3	7
Sympathetic understanding of personal problems	9	3
Job security	2	4
Interesting work	5	6

they wanted most from their jobs were rated by supervisors as least important. This suggests very little sensitivity by supervisors as to what things are really most important to workers.

By and large supervisors act as though incentives directed at satisfying physiological and safety motives are most important to their workers. Therefore, they tend to use the old reliable incentives—money, fringe benefits, and security—to motivate workers. But such studies when replicated periodically over the last several decades as part of management training programmes, have found similar results in the perception of managers. With the economic decline of the 1990s, "good wages" and "job security" have once again become high-strength needs for workers. It is thus important that managers know the tremendous discrepancies that seemed to exist in the past between what they thought workers wanted from their jobs and what workers said they really wanted.

From extensive research on incentive pay schemes, William F. Whyte found that money, the old reliable motivation tool, is not as almighty as it is supposed to be, particularly for production workers.

Another key factor as Mayo discovered, is their work group. Using the ratio of high-producing rate busters to low-producing restrictors as an index, Whyte estimated that only about 10% of the production workers in the U.S. ignore group pressure and produce as much as possible in response to an incentive plan. Thus it seems that even though workers are interested in advancing their own financial position, there are many other considerations—such as opinions of their fellow workers, their comfort and enjoyment on their jobs, and their long range security—that prevent them from making a direct, automatic, positive response to an incentive plan.

The most subtle and important characteristic of money is its power as a symbol. Its most obvious symbolic power is its market value. It is what money can buy, not money itself that gives it value. And because money has no intrinsic meaning of its own, it can symbolise almost any need an individual wants it to represent. In other words, money can mean what people want it to mean. Thus its use must be tailored to each employee's values. In this context, for money to motivate, three considerations must be met—one, the employee must have a high "net" preference for money i.e. the positive motivating effects of more pay must be greater than the negative effects of undesirable hours. Second, there needs to be a direct relationship between money and performance that the employee can perceive. If performance increases, then pay should increase and vice-versa. Third, there needs to be a direct relationship between effort and performance. If the effort increases, the performance should increase. Both the costs and benefits in this approach need to be determined, but overall it has a sound motivational base. In the context of today's financial burdens, a dramatic change in people's attitude toward work has been found as compared to in the sixties, in Herzberg's research years. Today financial reasons are the single most important reason or why people work. There is a motivational message here. If you want to increase money's power as a motivator, implement an incentive plan. The extra money will be a powerful motivator because it will be spent on high-value "extra" items!

It is important to know that you may as well have given the incentive/ reward system top marks, but the effectiveness of this as a motivator depends largely on the capabilities of those who run the system. Rewards don't work by themselves; they have to be managed carefully. Creating a situation where teams work effectively together in agreeing and achieving goals can be a good way of improving individual motivation.

Finally, it has to be recognised that some people will be self-motivated—they set themselves targets and then go for them—while with others, the motivational drive will be much lower. People in the former category may not need to be motivated by the management but they should still be rewarded appropriately in line with their contribution or they will rapidly become demotivated and go to a company where their talents will be properly recognised. Those in the latter category will need encouragement with incentives and rewards which are focussed on their particular needs.

■ ■ ■

Do You Like Your Job?

Understanding individual behaviour in an organisation requires knowing something about the influences that tend to make a person behave in a particular situation. Most often, the prerequisites for this are essentially psychological in nature—such as the employee's attitude towards the place of work, his perceptions regarding the role he is to perform in his organisation and the organisational climate in which he works. These, in turn, directly or indirectly affect the level of job satisfaction, organisational commitment, and general satisfaction of the individual within the organisation. Of late, researchers like Likert have clearly brought out that an integration of the individual's needs within his personality structure and that of the organisation in which he works is possible to far greater degree than ever imagined before. Such a view is drastically different from the traditional beliefs that organisational and individual needs are incompatible. Rabinowitz and Hall in their research work have shown that there is a definite interplay of a whole lot of factors such as the personality, organisational and communicative factors that operate in a very subtle manner to influence the organisational behaviour of an employee. One of the most affected factors in this context is job satisfaction, which is taken to be an attitude of employee reflecting the degree to which his important needs are satisfied by his job.

From an early stage, surveyors of employee's morale etc. have asked employees whether they were free of occupational stress and were satisfied with their jobs. Answers to such queries are assumed to reflect an internal state of the job holder. Psychologists like Schaffer, Adams, Lawler, Cooper, Herzberg and Vroom have proposed various theories to study the dynamics of this phenomenon. Their integration reveals that it is the global view in which the employee perceives his job and its assets and liabilities and that the bond between the two is essentially of a psychological nature, wherein the individual differences play the major role in terms of subjective need patterns, motivation patterns and perceptions of the worker, whereby he tries to gauge the gap between the actual and his desired perception about his job.

The following quiz describes the important elements that usually make up a job satisfaction measure. Give your feeling about your job by replying to each statement on the following levels of your satisfaction:

Very Much Satisfied 6
Much Satisfied 5
Somewhat Satisfied 4
Somewhat Dissatisfied 3
Much Dissatisfied 2
Very Much Dissatisfied 1

How do you feel about:

1. The way information flows around in your organisation.
2. Your relationship with other people at work.
3. The way you and your efforts are valued.
4. The nature of your job.
5. The degree to which you feel motivated by your job.
6. Career opportunities offered by your job.
7. The level of job security in your present job.
8. The extent to which you identify with the goals of your organisation.
9. The style of supervision used by your superiors.
10. The way changes and innovations are implemented in your job.
11. The kind of work or tasks that you are required to perform.
12. The degree to which you feel that you can personally grow in your job.
13. The manner in which conflicts are resolved in your organisation.
14. The scope your job provides to help you achieve your aspirations and ambitions.
15. The amount of participation which you are given in important decision making.
16. The degree to which your job taps the range of skills which you feel you possess.
17. The amount of flexibility and freedom you feel you have in your job.

18. The psychological 'feel' or climate that dominates your organisation.
19. Your level of salary relative to your experience.
20. The design or shape of your organisation's structure.
21. The amount of work you are given to do, whether too much or too little.
22. The degree to which you feel extended in your job.

Interpretation

90-132: Minimum Occupational Stress.

Your job seems to provide you ample opportunity to make the best of your capabilities and thereby get a sense of achievement. You must consider yourself to be one of the very few who are lucky enough to intrinsically enjoy their work. Keep it up.

45-89: Medium Occupational Stress.

Your work provides you a considerable amount of space to show your calibre without much job stress. You can further adapt yourself to it by sticking carefully to your work goals and time schedules.

1-44: Maximum Occupational Stress.

To combat your job stress, you have to adopt a skilful strategy of fixing up your work priorities and time management. Develop a mind set to like your work and cultivate a strong need for achievement motivation to accomplish your work targets to the best of your capabilities. Enhance your skills, if need be, by attending on-job training workshops and courses. Have a positive attitude towards your employer and colleagues and interact intelligently to seek clarities and job enrichment whenever you are faced with a block related to your job role or job performance. A belief in the dignity of your work will go a long way in providing you happiness and satisfaction.

■ ■ ■

Are You Gender-friendly at Work

How many times have you heard a Human Resource (HR) manager flaunting his company's credentials of being an equal employer, yet a minute later making some snide judgmental remark about a woman colleague?

Several times? Yes, it happens. No matter how much we may have evolved in other behavioural patterns, certain things are still resistant to change—patriarchy, for one. Following are a set of questions for male bosses and co-workers to ponder over and introspect on how they treat their women colleagues and whether it is necessary for them to make adjustments.

Tick Mark on Your Choice of Options for the Following Questions:

1. Do you perceive your contemporary female co-worker as:
    a) An individual
    b) As a woman
2. Would you assign an urgent, demanding time-bound and responsible assignment to your female worker?
    a) Yes
    b) No
3. Would you unhesitatingly assign an assignment to your woman subordinate which requires several decisions to be taken on her own?
    a) Yes
    b) No
4. If you have to give an incentive for the best worker would you:
    a) Give it to the best worker, irrespective of gender.
    b) Grant special advantage to a woman worker just because she has a comparative advantage of being a woman.
5. If you feel that a new woman subordinate is trying to please you with her feminine charm and boosts your ego with tact

and flattery, would you like to discourage this beyond a certain point or allow her to continue doing so?
a) Discourage and stop
b) Continue

6. Do you have the faith in you that a subordinate woman worker will come up to your expectation like her male counterparts in all job situations?
a) Yes
b) No

7. Do you tend to treat a woman boss with the same respect and awe as you do in case of your male boss?
a) Yes
b) No

8. Do you tend to feel threatened and insecure in your career when your competitor for the next promotion happens to be a woman and not a man?
a) Yes
b) No

9. In your conversation with female colleagues do you tend to gradually let it turn into loose talk?
a) Yes
b) No

10. Do you tend to prefer to encourage and promote (consciously or unconsciously) those female workers who are always willing to pay attendance to you and share personalized issues in their conversation with you, over other women workers?
a) Yes
b) No

11. If a particular assignment requires the services of a woman, would you like to encourage and insist on her working beyond office hours and ensure that she gets transport facilities to commute back home safely after the late night working hours?
a) Yes
b) No

12. Do you often approach female co-workers with a smiling face but are critical of their ability and capacities in their work, while discussing them with your male contemporaries?
a) Yes

b) No

13. Do you openly appreciate a female worker who has some original ideas concerning your organization's policies and methods of working even if it deviates to a great extent from your own view point?
a) Yes
b) No

Correct Answers

1. a), 2. a), 3. a), 4. a), 5. a), 6. a), 7. a), 8. b), 9. b), 10. b), 11. a), 12. b), 13. a)

Interpretation

9-13: You have an immense contribution in developing a congenial work environment for improving efficiency as well as the personal growth of female work force of your organization. They in return hold you in high esteem and regard you as a capable and efficient organisation man.

5-8: You are reasonably progressive and provide a comfortable work environment for the female work-force but you need to introspect as to how to create a work-environment in which their competencies and capabilities can be fostered further.

1-4: You tend to be prejudiced and biased and governed only by your personal life experiences. Education and status has not made any basic changes in your conventional attitudes towards women. You require a thorough introspection to improve the same so that you are surrounded by a more competent woman work force rather than a sloppy, flattering and inefficient one.

■ ■ ■

How Creative Are You?

Creativity enables individuals in organizations to be self-reliant, resourceful and confident for facing personal, interpersonal and other problems pertaining to work situations. Creativity is a trait of an individual which enhances one's capability to perceive a clue to a higher degree of synthesis even in conceptual ambiguity. It was once widely held to be limited to a few talented individuals. However, an impressive body of solid research over the past few decades has conclusively proved that most of us were born with rich and vigorous imaginations, and that creative ability is almost universally distributed. Creativity as a fundamental trait is possessed by every person and yet very few people make use of their creative potential. It includes being independent and spontaneous in expression, innovativeness, resourcefulness, and possessing problem solving aptitude.

Researches of psychologists Knecheges & Woods and Raudsepp and Hough, in the 1970's offer support to this notion by stating that creativity is contingent upon the preservation of the curiosity and wonder we had in early childhood and that unfortunately is the one thing that is conspicuous by its absence in most grown ups.

The big question then is, "what helps or hinders creativity?" Over time as one crosses childhood the inhibition of creativity increases as one conforms to the social pressure of the educational process and interacts in society. Eventually layers of behaviour are developed which thwart the creative potential. The spark of creativity shrinks and shrinks until no radiation emits from it. If this spark or energy is not challenged or is restricted, this confinement becomes tighter until the spark is finally extinguished.

However, by restraining ourselves to unstifle creativity, we can unearth our hidden potentials, and bring them to surface again to make use of them for a more creative and fulfilling life.

Are there some blocks – perceptual, emotional or cultural which you think tend to hinder your creativity? Take the following quiz and assess the barriers in your psyche which tend to hinder your creativity. The main barriers could be related to:

1. Your concept of Self — i.e. your self-esteem, self-confidence, handling of rejection, and ability to confront differing opinions.
2. Your need for Conformity — i.e. your inclination to break away from tried and true patterns, to take risks, to express your ideas and to scrutinize traditional values.
3. Your ability to handle the abstract — i.e. your tendencies to use the unconscious mind, to abstract, to view things in holistic ways and to rely on gut feelings or intuition.
4. Your ability for task achievement — i.e. your work patterns, persistence, attitude towards others, and resourcefulness.

Now read the following statements of this quiz and refer to the following scale and decide which numbers correspond to your level of agreement with the statement. Then write that number in the blank to the left of the statement.

1 – Strongly Agree
2 – Agree
3 – Agree Somewhat
4 – Disagree Somewhat
5 – Disagree
6 – Strongly Disagree

1. I evaluate criticism to determine how it can be useful to me.
2. When solving problems, I attempt to apply new concepts or methods.
3. I can shift gears or change emphasis in the abstract.
4. I always give a problem my best effort, even if it seems trivial or fails to arouse enthusiasm.
5. It is not difficult for me to have my ideas criticized.
6. In the past I have taken calculated risks and I would do so again.
7. I dream, daydream and fantasize easily.
8. Occasionally I try a so called "unworkable" answer and hope that it will prove to be workable.

9. I feel at ease with my colleagues even when my ideas or plans meet with public criticism or rejection.
10. I frequently read opinions contrary to my own to learn what the opposition is thinking.
11. I translate symbols into concrete ideas or action steps.
12. In the idea – formulation stage of a project, I withhold critical judgement.
13. I would modify any idea, plan or design, even if doing so would meet with opposition.
14. I feel comfortable in expressing my ideas even if they are in the minority.
15. I enjoy participating in non-verbal, symbolic or visual activities.
16. I keep a file of discarded ideas.
17. I would feel no serious loss of status or prestige if the management publicly rejected my plan.
18. I frequently question the policies, objectives, values or ideas of an organization.
19. I deliberately exercise my visual and symbolic skills in order to strengthen them.
20. I seldom reject ambiguous ideas that are not directly related to the problem.
21. I feel uncomfortable making waves for a worthwhile idea if it threatens the inner harmony of a group.
22. I am willing to present a truly original approach even if there is a chance it could fail.
23. I can recognize the times when symbolism or visualization would work best for me.

A	B	C	D
1	2	3	4
5	6	7	8
9	10	11	12
13	14	15	16
17	18	19	20
21	22	23	24

Columns Total _____   _____   _____

24. In the past I have determined when to leave an undesirable environment and when to stay and change the environment (including self-growth).

Now transfer your inventory responses to the appropriate blanks provided below, and then add the numbers in each column, and record the totals in the blanks provided:

Plot the scores from your scoring sheet onto the following graph. The vertical axis which represents your numbered scores, range from 6 to 24. The horizontal axis, which represents the columns on your scoring sheet, ranges from A to D. The key at the bottom identifies the barriers in each column. Connect the points you have plotted with a line. *The high points represent your barriers.* So try and work on those areas to eliminate their hindrance to your creativity.

24				
20				
15				
10				
6				
	A	B	C	D

Key to Barriers

    A = Barriers related to Self–confidence and Risk Taking.
    B = Barriers related to Need for Conformity.
    C = Barriers related to Use of the Abstract.
    D = Barriers related to Task Achievement.

■ ■ ■

How Well Do You Interact Within Your Workgroup?

Most people find it difficult to work and interact in an environment which is alien to them or with people of cultural preferences different from their own. The ways in which we feel, think, and behave can be checked in terms of how others perceive and interact with us.

As we develop within our cultures and in interactions with others, we tend to form preferences and various aspects of interpersonal interactions. Many of these preferences are identified in terms of 'context'. Two basic 'contexts' are termed as *individualistic* and *collectivistic*. The context in which one interacts affects how one relates to others, communicates, interprets information and so on, which in turn affects his worklife.

If you wish to gain self-awareness as regards which of the above two 'contexts' you belong to, read the following statements which describe how you might interact within a work or problem-solving group. Respond to each statement by ticking the option that best describes your preference, in terms of how strongly you agree or disagree with the statement. Use the following scoring method for assigning scores to your answers:

Strongly Disagree (SD) = 0
Disagree (D) = 1
Mildly Disagree (MD) = 2
Mildly Agree (MA) = 3
Agree (A) = 4
Strongly Agree (SA) = 5

Statements

(SD) (D) (MD) (MA) (A) (SA)
1. I would compromise with others in order to maintain harmony in the group.

(SD) (D) (MD) (MA) (A) (SA)
2. I would expect the team leader to direct members away from problems or issues that would upset the balance of the group.

(SD) (D) (MD) (MA) (A) (SA)
3. I would trust the group members and support their shared interests even if I don't agree with them.

(SD) (D) (MD) (MA) (A) (SA)
4. I would use the utmost diplomacy in order not to embarrass anyone while working through problems in the group.

(SD) (D) (MD) (MA) (A) (SA)
5. Once a commitment has the group's approval, it is expected to be honoured.

(SD) (D) (MD) (MA) (A) (SA)
6. I would decide on my own what should be done and how it should be done.

(SD) (D) (MD) (MA) (A) (SA)
7. I would direct others towards getting results as soon as possible.

(SD) (D) (MD) (MA) (A) (SA)
8. I would directly confront problems or conflicts between individuals in the group.

(SD) (D) (MD) (MA) (A) (SA)
9. I would say what I thought, even though it may hurt others' feelings.

(SD) (D) (MD) (MA) (A) (SA)
10. I would want outstanding individual performers in group activities rewarded more than those who did not contribute as much.

(SD) (D) (MD) (MA) (A) (SA)
11. I don't like doing work on my own or being separate from the group.

(SD) (D) (MD) (MA) (A) (SA)
12. I feel uncomfortable when there are individuals in the group who remain distant and don't interact with the group.

(SD) (D) (MD) (MA) (A) (SA)
13. In a group meeting it is important that we stay close together.

(SD) (D) (MD) (MA) (A) (SA)
14. It is best to have the leader in a centralised location where all

members of the group can interact with him or her.
(SD) (D) (MD) (MA) (A) (SA)
15. The best way to work in a group is to stay together in the same room until agreement is reached.
(SD) (D) (MD) (MA) (A) (SA)
16. I don't want to be interrupted when I'm working on or thinking about a problem.
(SD) (D) (MD) (MA) (A) (SA)
17. I need to be away from the group in order to think or make a decision.
(SD) (D) (MD) (MA) (A) (SA)
18. I prefer to work alone until I'm ready to get with the group.
(SD) (D) (MD) (MA) (A) (SA)
19. The leader of a group or organisation needs to be separate but where I can go to him/her when I need to.
(SD) (D) (MD) (MA) (A) (SA)
20. When working in a group, I prefer to work with individuals who think as I do.

Scoring

Convert each rating that you gave to a statement by assigning it a score as described above and place that score in the appropriate space as under:

Group A (denoting 'Collectivists')		Group B (denoting 'Individualists')	
Statements	Score	Statements	Score
1.		11.	
2.		12.	
3.		13.	
4.		14.	
5.		15.	
6.		16.	
7.		17.	
8.		18.	
9.		19.	
10.		20.	

Your Maximum obtainable score could be 100.

Interpretation

If you rank higher on statements belonging to :

The Group A (The Collectivist)

You tend to be a Collectivist. Collectivistic individuals place emphasis on relationships, group goals, the process and surrounding circumstances, verbal communication and interrelationships. Cultural norms are primarily group oriented. Family and community ties are strong; religions and spiritual beliefs are deep. In such a culture, people look beyond the obvious to note nuances in meaning, non-verbal communication cues, and the status of others.

Since you tend to belong to this group, your personal characteristics include being indirect, affiliative, informal, team-oriented, loyal, systematic, quiet, patient, dependable, cooperative, sharing, somewhat slow in making decisions, respectful and a good listener. You are more likely to downplay your own goals in favour of the goals of the group and are more committed to group agreements.

The Group B (The Individualist)

You are one of the individualistic people who focus on individualistic goals, tasks, facts, solutions, time-management and privacy. Individualists are assertive, directive, controlling, result-oriented, independent, strong-willed, competitive, quick to make decisions, impatient, organised, self-contained and have a high need to be recognised for their performance. Their goals are action-oriented to produce short-term material profits, and financial success is esteemed. Emotions are considered inappropriate in most social and work settings. Individualists' plans are progressive and can be changed quickly.

However such individuals can create less cohesion and stability in a group. They tend to be less committed to group agreements, and when there is a conflict between an individual's goals and those of the group, the individual's goals are of major importance. Individualists do not like to have to consider the opinions of others before they act. Clearing their plans with others interferes too much with their desire "to do their own thing".

Individual Application

If you score very high on either A or B group and very low on A or B group, you possess lower ability to interact across cultural context and may interact well with only those who have profiles *similar to yours*, but not with others.

If your scores are relatively high on both A and B groups, you possess higher ability to interact within groups in which there are varying levels of contextual requirements. You are better able to move *between* situations and/or groups with ease, to be more flexible and adaptable in interpretation and decision-making situations and to be more responsive in learning and decision-making.

In general, low scores represent a potential difficulty in interacting across groups with variations in cultural preferences. Language, religion, philosophical and other communication or social barriers are not included in this profile.

■ ■ ■

Can You Get to Open-up Others?

Some of us seem to be born with the qualities of trustworthiness and a basic warm disposition. In contrast, there are others who seem to have difficulty developing it partly because they've grown up in families lacking warmth and intimacy. Consequently, they feel uneasy when people get close to them. Some individuals grow in love and understanding with others and eventually achieve a satisfying relationship despite their backgrounds and shortcomings. People tend to confide in them without the fear of betrayal as they feel they are accepted by them in totality, as they are, and can count on them in times of need. The sensitivity in them to the feelings and reactions of others makes them somewhat indispensable. They seem to share an attitude similarity and affinity with others, which often bestows a lot of popularity to them. They are high self-monitors and modify their own behaviour in order to make a favourable impression on others.

Should you like considering the flavour of this self-monitoring dimension in you, contemplate on the following issues and see where you stand.

Answer the question with an honest "Yes" or "No".

1. Do people frequently like to tell you about themselves?
2. Have you been told that you are a good listener?
3. Do you possess the quality of accepting others spontaneously?
4. Do people trust you with their secrets?
5. Do you easily get people to open up?
6. Do people tend to feel relaxed around you?
7. Do you enjoy listening to people?
8. Are you generally sympathetic to people's problems?
9. Do you encourage people to tell you how they are feeling?
10. Can you keep people talking about themselves?

11. Can you empathise with people who tell you their problems?
12. Do people consider you as a trustworthy and genuine person?
13. Do you make an effort at a 'healing touch' with your comforting words as you communicate with people?
14. Do you appear altruistic to others?
15. Do you look to the brighter side of things and practise positive thinking?

Scoring

Assign one mark for every **'Yes'** answer.

Interpretation

11-15: You are a stimulating and highly self-monitored personality, with a genuine concern for others and take pains to give them a patient hearing. You are able to influence the impression you make on others and read the reactions of others. People look up to you with trust and your listening and interpersonal skills make you one of the most sought after persons in your circle of friends. Your personal effectiveness and art of winning friends and influencing people cause you a great deal of popularity.

6-10: You tend to be moderately inclined towards your fellowmen who seek comfort and solace for their trouble zones from you in their times of stress. You seem to possess a fair knack of enrolling others into opening up their distressed feelings to you. Your capacity to share others' grief and get them to let off their emotional steam acts therapeutically for them.

1-5: Your self-centred approach and a lack of interest in others hold them back from opening up to you. Your lack of communication with others seems to cause this gap. This failure in intimate communication and a genuine interest in others tends to occur at a deeper level of sharing feelings, expectations, intentions and personal needs. It's high time you got aware of the essentials of sharing love and close relationships in life. True commitment to life often lies in selfless love and companionship and their subtle rewards.

■ ■ ■

Are You A Good Listener?

People everywhere love to be listened to, and they almost always respond to others who listen to them. Organisational research reveals that no manager is more persuasive than a good listener. "Active listening is the single most important of all communication skills. More important than stirring oratory. More important than a powerful voice. More important than the ability to speak multiple languages. More important even than a flair for the written word", says Dale Carnegie.

It's surprising how few people listen really well, but successful leaders, more often than not, are the ones who have learned the value of listening. This means listening to employees, to customers, and to your friends and family—even to what your harshest critics have to say. Surely, it does not mean becoming a captive of other people's opinions but it does mean hearing them out.

Active listening requires an immense involvement in the conversation, even when the listener's lips are still. It requires genuine engagement. And it demands some kind of response—quick, thoughtful, on target and concise.

"A person who's actively listening", says Bill Makahilahila, Director of Human Resources at SGS-Thomson microelectronics, Inc., "is usually the one who is asking questions and then waiting for a response, as opposed to coming up with an instant solution. Active listening is occurring when the employee feels and knows beyond a shadow of doubt that you're not jumping to conclusions." Further, Makahilahila thinks this is such an important concept that he has even created an Active listening Award for SGS-Thomson supervisors who excel at listening.

The first step to becoming a strong, active listener is to understand how important good listening is. The second step is wanting to learn. Finally, you have to practise those budding listening skills, for it is not just listening, but internalising other people's feelings and thinking about them. Then being able to mirror them back; so you can demonstrate their importance to you.

Strangely enough, listening to someone else's opinions is often the best method of getting them around to *your* way of thinking. Listening is the way to persuade others with your ears! It's true; listening can be a tremendously powerful tool for convincing others to see the world the way you do.

"The real key" says merchant banker Tom Saunders, of Saunders Karp & Company, "is getting to understand a person and what he values and how he wants to look at investments and whether or not you could honestly say your approach was right and compatible for him."

Saunders is in the business of advising big corporations about how to invest prodigious sums of money. His number one technique? Listening to them. It all "goes back to listening", he says. "What was really on his mind? Why had he said no? What was the real reason behind it? "I've had a twenty-five year relationship with AT&T, which has just been extraordinary. I think it's all basically been due to listening."

Are you too adept at this art of turning listening into a practical improvement tool? Answer the following quiz—

As you listen:

1. Do you ask questions and wait for an answer?
2. Do you respond quickly and directly to the questions that are asked?
3. Does the other person *feel* that you are listening actively to him/her?
4. Do you give an occasional nod, or an 'uh-huh' or an "I see" while you listen?
5. Do you shift your posture or lean forward in the chair and at appropriate moments smile or shake your head meaningfully while you listen?
6. Do you maintain strong eye contact with your conversation mate?

7. Do you go ahead and ask a question that follows closely from what was just said *after* the other person comes to a break in his or her talking?
8. Are you mentally "with your speaker" every moment?
9. Are you tempted to interrupt the speaker in between if you disagree with him on an issue?
10. Do you listen patiently with an open mind?
11. Do you encourage your speaker to express his ideas fully?
12. As a listener are you able to take time away from your most important focus yourself?

Scoring

Correct answers: 'Yes' answers for all questions except no. 9 are correct answers.

Interpretation

8 and above: You really are a "people's person". You are a good listener and intelligent enough to understand that listening intently to people is one of the highest compliments we can pay anyone. So, you have others think of you as really interested in them when in reality you simply listen to them and encourage them to talk. This way you learn things and people respond to you since you listen to them. You are thus an effective communicator and can become a successful leader. Keep it up!

Less than 8: You seem to be too preoccupied with your own self to listen. Come out of your self-centred approach. You have to learn to listen to others—your employees, customers, friends, family as well as your critics. Get involved in others. People must be treated as individuals. They're people first, employees second. This is a special motivation technique. So get set and step outside yourself to discover what's important to someone else.

■ ■ ■

The Self-actualization Approach

Psychologists such as Abraham Maslow, hold that some people tend to reach a healthier, more optimal level of functioning than the average person. He called them self-actualized people. Such people are relatively free from major psychological problems and have made the best possible use of their talents and strengths. Compared to the average person, these people have certain characteristics in common, such as continued freshness of appreciation of everyday realities; greater acceptance of themselves and others, high creativity and high resistance to conformity. Many people fail to actualize themselves because of the lack of supportive circumstances. However, countless people have been significantly creative despite deprived circumstances. Maslow acknowledged that it is something of a mystery why affluence releases some people for growth while stunting others. Hence a favourable environment alone is not enough to ensure growth. Individuals must also have an intense desire to grow, to offset the apathy and resistance to growth. All things considered, personal development tends to be a struggle between growth-fostering and growth-discouraging forces.

To assess your own level of psychological growth and self-actualization, indicate your agreement or disagreement with each of the following statements by placing the appropriate number in the blanks before each item. Assign your scores as follows—1=Disagree, 2=Somewhat Disagree, 3=Somewhat Agree, 4=Agree.

1. I do not feel ashamed of any of my emotions. —
2. I feel I must do what others expect me to do. —
3. I believe that people are essentially good and can be trusted. —
4. I feel free to be angry at those I love. —
5. It is always necessary that others approve of what I do. —
6. I find it difficult to accept my weaknesses. —

7. I can like people without having to approve of them. —
8. I fear failure. —
9. I avoid attempts to analyze and simplify complex domains. —
10. It is better to be yourself than to be popular. —
11. I have no mission in life to which I feel especially dedicated. —
12. I can express my feelings even when they might result in undesirable consequences. —
13. I do not feel particularly responsible to help anybody. —
14. I am bothered by fears of being inadequate. —
15. I am loved because I give love. —

Scoring

To get your score, responses placed before items 2, 5, 6, 8, 9, 11, 13, 14 should be reversed (4=1, 3=2, 2=3, 1=4). Then add the resulting numbers to the responses of the rest of the items. Your total score can range between 15-60.

Interpretation

High Score (47-60)

You are a highly self-actualized individual who tends to live in the present rather than in the guilt and regret of the past, or with over-idealized goals and fears of the future. You also tend to be inner-directed, extraverted, and rational in your thoughts and behaviours. You make choices by taking reasonable risks rather than by sticking with the safe and secure. You are open to new experiences and trust your own experience.

Average Score (31-46)

You have a fair ability for perceiving and experiencing yourself in relation to your environment. You realize that you begin to live authentically only as you affirm your inherent human freedom and take responsibility for your lives. You are aware that self-actualization is more of a life-long process that enhances the meaning of life rather than a readily attainable goal.

Low Score (15-30)

Your inner core of growth seems to be relatively weak and underdeveloped and is really stifled by disturbing circumstances. Know that it is your decisions, not conditions that determine your destiny. Small improvements are believable, hence achievable. Nothing splendid has ever been achieved except by those who dared believe that something inside them is superior to circumstances.

■ ■ ■

Success or Failure at Work

Could you define success categorically? It means different things to different people. Success for the surgeon means saving a life. Success for a sick person means restored health. Success can be in coping with unusual problems. It can be in acquiring more money or material things, particularly in the present era.

According to Sidney, a noted psychologist " Whatever you are by nature, keep to it. Never desert your line of talent. Be what Nature intended you for, and you will succeed."

Although modern civilization has made remarkable progress in many fields, it has all the same neglected others that are vital for well being. "Material progress does indicate success and improves well-being upto a point, but beyond that point instead of lifting us upward, it only leads us around in circles", says Eknath Easwaran in his book Discovering Your Hidden Spiritual Resources.

Unfortunately, the modern man tends to seek joy through sensual aggrandisement which inevitably turns out to be a short lived affair and at times a painful experience. He does not care to attain real success in perfecting the art of looking within for joy which is everlasting and sans any trace of any pain or sorrow. As in the sacred *Bhagwad Gita*, Lord Krishna tells Arjuna, "He who enjoys the happiness of the self does not care for any power." On the contrary, the modern man in a great hurry to attain success in acquiring wealth, fame, power and pleasure does not seem to care for the happiness of the self. And one is often reminded of the meaningful couplet, "What is this life if full of care, one has no time to stand and stare." Ironically that is the price paid for apparent success. Such a success is nothing but failure in reality. In the words of Robert H. Schuller, author of Success is Never Ending, Failure is Never Final, failure is in "yielding to cowardice in the face of an urgent but risky venture; in retreating from a high calling to a noble duty because you fear imperfection in the execution of that duty. It's in protecting your pride from a possibly embarrassing professional failure rather than promoting a wonderful and worthy cause. It's in demoting faith from the leadership of your life and promoting fear to a position of power." This is real failure as a person, though apparently it may mean success in material terms.

What does success mean to you personally? Reflect over the following statements and see if you find yourself agreeing/disagreeing with them.

1. Success comprises not merely in terms of worldly or material success but possessing humanistic qualities as well such as love for others, honesty, humility, forgiveness, empathy for others, steadfastness, self-control and compassion to living beings.
2. Success means not just possessing powers for dominating, controlling and commanding others but being humble and having the spirit of service and self-sacrifice.
3. Success means that despite the worldly engagements, chalking out a programe of life—drawing your spiritual routine and sticking to it systematically and regularly.
4. Success may or may not mean that you've acquired a lot. It does not mean that you have become a generous person.
5. Success is noblest when it leaves you with the self-respect that you have been a good steward of the life, liberties and opportunities that God offered to you.
6. Success is building your own self-respect by affirming the dignity of your fellow human beings—having great hearts and super souls and being admired, respected and loved by them even though your material acquisitions may be modest.
7. Success is to do something good when you can, where you can, while you can.
8. Success is to become a Possibility Thinker—to dare to dream the impossible dream with God and to give Him a chance to make this dream come true.
9. Success is never ending. It dies as soon as it becomes static. It continues to produce new possibilities, sometimes in the form of new problems. Failure is never final.
10. Achievers may lose their jobs, get rejected, watch their companies fail or see their ideas flounder but they take

advantage of adversity, carving opportunities from change.
11. Successful people radiate a positive attitude that inspires others to help them realize their dreams.
12. Successful people know that being persistent involves making choices. And choice involves risk, which they willingly undertake.
13. Successful people understand that no one makes to the top in a single-bound. What truly sets them apart is their willingness to putting one step in front of the other in spite of adversity.

Scoring

Assign one mark for every **'yes'** answer.

Interpretation

Your understanding of the art of living successfully is as under:
9-13: Excellent
5-8: Fair
1-4: Poor

■ ■ ■

Take A Peep into Your Value Orientation

"If you compare yourself
With others in your profession
You may become vain and bitter
For always there will be
Greater or lesser persons than yourself.
Enjoy your achievements as well as your plans
And keep interested
In your own career, however humble,
For it is a real possession
In the changing fortunes of time."

— ***Saint Paul***

Values, such as these lend us emotional intelligence and an inner psychological stability which goes a long way in granting us success in our career endeavours. Personal strategic planning forms an important part of HRD programmes today. It is the process by which you create a vision of your future and then determine specific steps to take to achieving that future. The process begins by clarifying values, writing your vision statements and then developing corresponding mission statements to translate your visions into a tangible reality. Values are an essential prerequisite for all this and in fact govern our missions, which in turn, grant us our cherished dreams-come-true.

Values, then, are concepts, principles or standards that drive our decisions and actions. Examples of values are honesty, persistence, dependability, self-sufficiency and faith. Without a clear awareness of one's core values which constitute a vision of the future, a person often renders himself directionless. Each one of us must examine and identify the values we want to live by, for they are our internal guideposts. They help us make the right decisions in our personal life as well as at crucial junctions of our career life. They shape us at the psychological plane and help us determine the society we will create tomorrow by deciding upon the values we emphasize today. They, in fact, empower us to work ethically and more fruitfully as they reflect themselves in our work styles and our work culture.

Most of us are psychologically and culturally conditioned in our value education. The understanding of the Self and our relationship with the cosmos is sadly missing in our formal education system. Experiential learning is often the ultimate answer to such an intellectual quest. When our introspection clarifies our values, we are better able to make wise choices, interact more effectively and end up being more creative in whatever we plan to do.

Following are a set of values (based on the model designed by Susan H. De Vogal at Minnesota) denoting different dimensions of organisational development value system. Read them carefully and examine as to which ones form an integral part of your value system Assign weightage to a statement as regards the extent to which it represents your thinking most of the time. Follow your initial instinct in assessing them. Assign weightage to each statement as under:

0 = Disagree
1 = Mildly Agree
2 = Agree
3 = Strongly Agree

1. I try to remain neutral when I encounter a client system's politics.
2. If there was some negative information discussed about certain people in the organisation, I refuse to share it with them.
3. I do not remain silent when I see evidence of gender discrimination or sexual harassment in a client organization.
4. I attend as many meetings of professional organizations as I can.
5. When a manager asks me for a feedback about his or her effectiveness, I give my honest views.
6. I try to remain neutral when I have friends in an organization.
7. I don't share personal information that I know about an employee, regardless of how I gained it.

8. I don't participate in organisational processes that will result in people losing their jobs.
9. I am willing to discuss my difficult cases with my colleagues.

Scoring Form: Transfer your scores of the assessed statements to this scoring form denoting different OD value dimensions:

OD value dimensions	Statements	Scores obtained
Objectivity and Independence	1	—
	6	—
	11	—
	16	—
	Total	—
Confidentiality	2	—
	7	—
	12	—
	17	—
	Total	—
Social Justice	3	—
	8	—
	13	—
	18	—
	Total	—
Professional Development	4	—
	9	—
	14	—
	19	—
	Total	—
Truthfulness	5	—
	10	—
15		—
	20	—
	Total	—

10. If I have doubts about the effectiveness of a requested or proposed intervention, I share those doubts with the clients.
11. I try to remain neutral when I get caught between conflicting emotional needs of organisational members.

12. I never share information when I have promised to keep it confidential.
13. I don't remain silent when I see evidence of discrimination against persons with differing abilities in a client organization.
14. Before I try a new intervention, I study the theory behind it.
15. When asked by a client about a specific intervention, I am truthful about whether or not I have ever tried it.
16. I insist on raising difficult issues, even if I know that doing so might jeopardize my contract or job.
17. If a manager asks me to gather information to help fire somebody, I refuse.
18. I do not hesitate to work with a client whose product or service conflicts with my personal views.
19. I do not keep silent when I see evidence of racism in a client organisation.
20. I disclose the risks of an intervention, even if I believe the potential benefits greatly outweigh the risks.

Interpretation

Compare your total scores for all the five value dimensions. The higher your total score for a particular value, the more important that value is to you. This may help you to understand the priorities you use in resolving ethical conflicts, particularly when you make choices between values that are important to you.

In case, you score very low on certain dimensions and very high on others, avoid such a lop-sided value system and try balancing it by cultivating the others as well.

■ ■ ■

Get An Aura

At some point of time in our lives, most of us have often felt intrigued or in awe of some powerful personality. We feel the instinctive attraction or repulsion for somebody and can often give no particular reasons for it. The successful preacher, doctor, singer or artist, whom we meet for the first time, seems to possess a magnetic personality — none the less, the attraction and repulsion speak of an intrinsic harmony or disharmony between each other's *auras* .

An aura is a kind of subtle extension of the personality...a magnetic emanation generated by the etheric and other forces of the being or the object with which it is connected. The aura is capable of giving and receiving impressions and through this medium we make conscious psychological contact apart from the physical senses.

Although western scholars Dr. Coates, Paracelsus and Van Helmont propagated the theory of the *Astral Body* ,and held that around the physical body extended an invisible radiation or 'fiery globe' , it was not until the eighteenth century that the modern scientific study of the aura began. The year 1734 symbolized mesmerism through the birth of Anton Mesmer who became one of the most ardent students of occultism of any period. Dr.W.J.Kilner., a Medical Electrician at St. Thomas's Hospital London, in his book *'The Human Atmosphere'* announced his discovery of a scientific method whereby the human atmosphere or "Aura" could be observed and read, which marked a new era for the Aura.

Using his auric sight through a specially designed screen excluding certain rays of light and rendering visible the ultra-violet Dr. Kilner studied various subjects under observation who stood against a black background in a dimly- lit room. He found out that every human being is surrounded by a faint, luminous , but colourless mist extending about 18 inches to 2feet in all directions and somewhat oval in shape . It varied in shape and clearness from day to day and appeared fainter and obscure in illness. Amazingly, a strong positive aura reacted upon the weak and negative kind as a fully charged battery will disseminate its charge if connected to weaker ones. In contrast a weak , depleted aura indicating reduced vitality, acted as a psychic sponge or "Vampire" on those around and sapped their energy. The human aura thus partakes the essential qualities of the etheric, the astral, the mental, and the spiritual forces of the individual. It explains why some people are a source of inspiration and personal power, influencing all those who come within the sphere of their influence.

Another interesting dimension to the study of aura is its colour. The aura is rendered the most complex and diversified by the varied play of the emotions, passions and feelings which impart a definite colour tone to the auric relations. Being the sum-total of thought-forces (etheric, astral, mental and spiritual) of the individual, it expresses itself in terms of varied colour vibrations .

Personality profiles and colours of the aura

It would perhaps be interesting to study human profiles, focussing on the colour of their auras, some of which are as under:

The Red Aura: Red being the symbol of life, signifies strength and vitality. People with a great deal of red in their auras have strong physical propensities, strong minds and wills, and usually a materialistic outlook in life .They often manifest a very warm and affectionate nature. Red also denotes the deepest of human passions—passionate love, courage, hatred, revenge etc.

The Orange Aura: It comprises all shades of orange from dull-reddish denoting selfishness and pride to the bright clear tones of health and vitality. Orange expresses the vital force, the energy of the sun.

The Yellow Aura: Except for certain dark, muddy shades, the golden shades particularly denote soul qualities and astral-mental forces. Yellow symbolizes thought and mental concentration and shows the presence of intellect, optimism and spiritualism.

The Green Aura: With the exception of olive green and certain dark shades, it indicates Individualism, Energy and Supply. It is the keynote of the ego. The green ray governs individual growth, like for example, the growing seed. People who have achieved prosperity and success in life, invariably display strong green tints in their auras. Bright, clear, green appears in the auras of people who are naturally animated, versatile, thoughtful and adaptable.

The Blue Aura: Heaven's own hue, it represents inspiration—the spiritual colour. In China and Japan it is considered the colour of Fortune. It signifies an artistic and harmonious nature and spiritual understanding. Bright blue denoting self-reliance and confidence, those with such an aura as a rule, are loyal friends and sincere characters.

The Violet Aura: It is rarely seen and is the most highly spiritual colour, indeed hardly belonging to the earth planet at all, but to the high sphere of spiritual being, denoting true greatness and worthiness. People remarkable for their selfless love and wisdom radiate beautiful violet colour tones. The more blue shades of purple are a sign of transcendental idealism.

The Black Aura: Strictly speaking black is not a colour, but a negation of colour, associated from ancient times with dark deeds and devilry, and its presence in the aura is always evil and vicious; denoting hatred, discord and evil thoughts of all types.

Reading Auras: If you are lucky to possess auric-clairvoyance and wish to develop auric-sight for reading auras, you can concentrate your sensing faculty on another person, choosing someone with whom you are in harmony. A dark curtain should be hung up in a quiet room on the wall opposite the window. Make him stand or sit about twelve or eighteen inches away from the dark curtain, with what little light is there falling evenly on him.

If it is the day time, stand at the window and gaze at the sky—not the sun—for half a minute; if night it will be sufficient to gaze at the electric light for the same length of time. Then closing your eyes, sit relaxed and endeavour to become as passive as possible. Concentrate mentally on the idea of the aura, without making an effort of will. Gaze calmly at the subject (the person) and note the formation of any mist, lights or rays in any region of his or her body. Do not, however be easily discouraged if nothing is seen.

Patient and regular practice is necessary in developing auric sight as any other form of psychic development. Colours in the aura are not always seen objectively, but they may be 'felt' or sensed.

Mysteries of the occult could thus enable you to profile a person's character—his passions, habits, ideas, aspirations, all that constitutes his physical, moral, intellectual and even biological existence…amazing isn't it?

■ ■ ■

What is Your Organization Type?

Organizations that we live in and work with are human creations and fundamentally they consist of people rather than buildings, equipment, machinery etc. They are fundamental to our well-being and productivity. The structure, technology and environment of the organisation influences human activity, and are interrelated in complex ways. They are in a sense living organisms with cultures, brains and complex systems, which create their own political systems, change, barriers and roles. It is essential that we understand the dynamics of an organisation, as well as its pattern, if we are to have accurate communications within it and make the most of its human resources.

Answer **"Yes" or "No" for each of the following statements** (modified from Manfred F.R. et al's inventory) depicting different organisational patterns A to E below. This would fathom the organisational type you are working in, along with its strengths and weaknesses and prescriptive strategies to be followed to fortify it.

Pattern A

1. Is power in your organisation highly centralised in the hands of the chief executive?
2. Is there a very strong oranisational culture in which everyone at the management level sees things in essentially the same way?
3. Does the chief executive seem overburdened with work because he or she tries to do everything himself?
4. Does the chief executive make decisions rapidly without consulting other people?
5. Are sycophants the main ones being promoted?
6. Does most of the information flow down rather than up the hierarchy?

Pattern B

1. Is there an atmosphere of suspicion and distrust in the organisation?
2. Do managers blame external "enemies" (regulators, government, and competitors) for the organisation's problems?
3. Are there organisational "spies" who inform top managers about what is happening at lower levels?
4. Is there much secrecy regarding performance information, salaries, decisions etc.?
5. Does the chief executive have a "siege mentality" constantly depending against perceived external attacks?
6. Is there a strong emphasis on management information systems to identify inadequacies and assign blames?

Pattern C

1. Is there a "leadership vacuum" in the organisation?
2. Is the chief executive too busy with outside matters to pay attention to the organisation and its business?
3. Does political infighting occur very often?
4. Is the organisation badly split, with much disagreement among the various functional areas or divisions?
5. Do decisions get delayed for a long period of time because of squabbling?
6. Are strategies badly fragmented, vacillating between one approach and another according to which senior manager is favoured by the executive?

Scoring

Determine which pattern collected the most "yes" responses. If you checked only one or two "yes" answers within a pattern, you probably *are not working* in that type of organisation. However, if you checked half or more "yes" responses within a pattern, you probably are working within that type of organisation.

Interpretation

Pattern A: "The Dramatic Organisation"
Characteristics

- Has strong leader who is idealised by subordinates.
- Has strong leader who is primary catalyst for the subordinates' morale and initiative.
- Exhibits very centralised policy making (in hands of impulsive, hyperactive leader)

Strengths

- Can create momentum needed to take organisation through start-up phase.
- Has ability to rebound after failures and ability to continue moving forward.
- Comes up with ideas to revitalise the organsiaiton.

Weaknesses

- Lacks a consisitent strategy.
- Sometimes lacks necessary controls.
- Tends to avoid consulting with, or getting feedbacks from, lower levels.

Prescriptions

- Plant both feet firmly on the ground
- Distribute authority—empowerment, delegation.
- Sharpen focus—get rid of worthless propositions.

Pattern B: "The Suspicious Organisation"
Characteristics

- Has fight-or-flight culture.
- Lacks trust—emphasis placed on intimidation and uniformity.
- Is reactive, conservative, overly analytical, secretive.

Strengths

- Shows good knowledge of events inside and outside the organization.
- Avoids dependence on a single market segment/customer.
- Provides positive opportunities for growth and diversification.

Weaknesses

- Lacks a consistent and concerted management strategy, falls victim to "groupthink".
- Has reactive, piecemeal, contradictory, distrustful atmosphere.
- Experiences high staff turnover because of insecurity and disenchantment.

Prescription
- Develop a unified strategy and sense of mission.
- Foster trust and break down communication barriers.
- Break down "policing" system.
- Establish a participative culture.
- Create distinctive competencies.
- Pursue strategy themes.

Pattern C: "The Detached Organisation"
Characteristics
- Lacks warmth and emotion.
- Engages in jockeying for power—lots of conflict and insecurity.
- Demonstrates strategic thinking dominated by indecisive, inconsistent, narrow perspectives.

Strenghts
- Has middle managers who play an active role.
- Shares variety of points of view in formulating strategies.
- Has individual mangers who take initiative.

Weaknesses
- Lacks leadership.
- Exhibits inconsistent or vacillating strategies.
- Decides issues by political negotiations rather than on the basis of facts.

Prescription
- Consider the whole.
- Get a senior manager willing to provide active leadership.
- Reward overall organisational performance.
- Create distinctive competencies.
- Establish active coordinating committees.

■ ■ ■

On Your Own
(Are you an entrepreneur?)

With the increasing opportunities for education which hold a promise of occupational mobility and the diversity of job opportunities as a result of industrialisation and urbanisation, a new social-economic environment conducive to entrepreneurship is emerging fast. Entrepreneurship refers to the general trend of setting up new enterprises in a society. An entrepreneur is innovative, has an urge to take risks in face of uncertainties and possesses an intuition. The emergence of entrepreneurs in a society depends upon closely interlinked economic, social, religious, cultural and psychological factors.

Entrepreneurial researchers suggest that the motives, attitudes and skills required to step into entrepreneurship need not be the same as those required to be a successful manager. An entrepreneurial manager requires not as much of a concern for excellence as a need to influence and lead others. Mc Clelland and Burnham's research reveals that an entrepreneurial manager should have a high need for influencing others (need power), a low need to establish emotional relationships (low need for affiliation) and a high capacity to discipline one's own self (inhibition).

Entrepreneurial motivation, sense of efficacy, moderate risk taking behaviour, openness to feed back and learning from experience, need for independence, hope for success and flexible authority relationship, are some other vital psychological factors for an entrepreneurial manager. Entrepreneurship, it is traditionally believed, is an inborn quality and entrepreneurs are born and not made. But recent researches and experiments in promoting Entrepreneurship have shown that it can be planned and developed through creating opportunities, providing facilities, giving incentives and studying the human factor—i.e. the individual, who responds to these external opportunities.

More than six hundred organisations/institutions in India are directly engaged in propagating, developing, promoting and conducting Entrepreneurship Development Programmes. Training has been the most important component of all these programmes. National institutions such as NIESBUD, New Delhi, and EDII, Ahmedabad conduct Accreditation Programmes for training Entrepreneurial Motivation Training Trainers.

Individuals with a high level of entrepreneurial internality have been found to possess more internal locus-of-control to sustain entrepreneurial activities, as compared to those with a more external (less entrepreneurial) locus-of-control orientation. The following quiz based on the trainers' trainings at NIESBUD measures your own orientation towards entrepreneurship.

Scoring

There are 10 pairs of statements In each pair you may agree with one statement more than the other. Tick mark only the statement (a or b) with which you agree more than the other one, for each pair.

1.a. Whether or not a salesperson will be able to sell his product depends on how effective the competitors are.
  b. No matter how good the competitors are, an effective salesperson will always be able to sell his product.
2.a. Capable entrepreneurs believe in planning their activities in advance.
  b. There is no need for advance planning, because no matter how enterprising one is, there always will be chance factors that influence success.
3.a. Whether or not a person can become a successful entrepreneur depends on social and economic conditions.
  b. Real entrepreneurs can always be successful, irrespective of social or economic conditions.
4.a. Entrepreneurs fail because of their own lack of ability and perceptiveness.
  b. Entrepreneurs are bound to fail at least half the time, because

success or failure depends on a number of factors beyond their control.
5.a. Entrepreneurs are often victims of forces they can neither understand nor control.
 b. By taking an active part in political, social and economic affairs, entrepreneurs can control events that affect their businesses.
6.a. When purchasing raw material or any other goods, it is always wise to collect as much information as possible from various sources and then make a final choice.
 b. There is no point in collecting a lot of information, in the long run, the more you pay, the better the product is.
7.a. These days, people must depend at every point on the support, help and mercy of others (governmental agencies, beaurocracies, banks etc.)
 b. It is possible to generate one's own income without depending too much on the bureaucracy. What is required is a knack in dealing with people.
8.a. The market situation toady is very unpredictable. Even perceptive entrepreneurs falter quite often.
 b. When an entrepreneur's prediction of the market situation is wrong, the person can blame only himself or herself in reading the market correctly.
9.a. There are many events beyond the control of entrepreneurs.
 b. Entrepreneurs are the creators of their own experiences.
10a. Organizational effectiveness can be achieved by employing competitive and effective people.
 b. No matter how competent employees in a company are, if socio-economic factors are not good, the organisation will have problems.

Interpretation

1 b; 2 a.; 3 b.; 4 a.; 5 b.; 6 a.; 7 b.; 8 b.; 9 b.; 10 a. denote an internal locus-of-control and a high entrepreneurial orientation.

■■■

Your Life-style Influences Your Work Output

Life-style Orientation of an employee is rapidly becoming a consideration at the organizational level. People of the present generation do not seem to respond to the same rewards and incentives as their predecessors did. While deciding to go in for a particular organization, employees give major consideration to its compatibility with their predominant life-style.

In depth organizational research of successful (fast upward movement) and less successful executives in well-known organizations have identified a number of factors associated with career and role success and failure. Two distinct patterns emerged from the groupings of these factors. The one associated with career success or job success was called "the enlarging style" and the other (associated with success) was called "the enfolding style."

Enlarging Style

The enlarging life style is oriented toward the goal of innovations, change, and growth. The enlarger moves away from the tradition and places emphasis on adaptation, self-development, and extension of influence outward, into the work and community spheres. He looks for responsibility on the job and is likely also to seek and achieve a position of influence in organisation. Self-development activities are stressed. Parental religions and peer group ties are weakened, as the enlargers find that their values have changed so dramatically that their career and self-development tend to occupy their highest priorities in life.

Enfolding Style

The enfolding style is oriented to the goals of tradition, stability and inward strength. They are drawn towards the familiar spheres, such as parental ties, and seek to keep a relationship active with childhood friends, if that is at all possible.

They find it upsetting to leave their hometown areas even if the move represents career advancement. They like to settle into a pursuit and see it through to a full conclusion, obtaining great satisfaction from a job well done.

The enfolder forms a close attachment to a small circle of friends and most of his or her socialising is done with relatives. Status consideration sometimes embarrasses and enfolders who value informality, sincerity and genuineness in human affairs more than high status.

Are you curious as to which category of style you belong? Then take the following quiz based on Bray, Campbell, and Grant's researches and do a bit of mental exercise to find out your predominant life-style.

Instructions for part A

Ask yourself how much time and energy you spent on each activity listed. Then decide that time and energy compares with the time and energy other members of your group (profession, occupation, etc.) are probably spending on that activity. Though you may not know exactly the time and energy spent by others, your perception is what is important in this quiz. Therefore, circle the number that seems to apply to you as follows:

Circle 1 if: You spend much less time and energy than the average for your group (i.e., your amounts of time and energy are among the lowest 5 percent).

Circle 2 if: You spend somewhat less time than the average for your group (i.e., your amounts are higher than the lowest 5 percent but still among the lowest 20 percent).

Circle 3 if: You spend about the same amount of time and energy as the average of your group (i.e., your amounts are among the middle 60 percent).

Circle 4 if: You spend somewhat more time and energy than the average for your group (your amounts are among the highest 20 percent but still lower than the top 5 percent).

Circle 5 if: You spend much more time and energy than the average for your group (your amounts are among the highest 5 percent)

Activity	Lowest 5%	Low 5%-20%	Middle 60%	High 5%-20%	Highest 20%
1. Reading to broaden knowledge.	1	2	3	4	5
2. Being with your spouse and children.	1	2	3	4	5
3. Exercising to improve physical fitness (swimming, jogging, etc.).	1	2	3	4	5
4. Attending courses for self-development.	1	2	3	4	5
5. Engaging in religious activities.	1	2	3	4	5
6. Engaging in spiritual pursuits or activities.	1	2	3	4	5
7. Acquiring financial assets (shares, real estate, etc.).	1	2	3	4	5
8. Dealing with problems/matters of your family members.	1	2	3	4	5
9. Contacting and meeting with friends and associates.	1	2	3	4	5
10. Engaging in leisure-oriented activities (hobbies, sports, etc.).	1	2	3	4	5
11. Socialising (at parties or clubs, with small groups, etc.).	1	2	3	4	5
12. Taking part in professional associations, societies, activities	1	2	3	4	5
13. Contributing to community service	1	2	3	4	5
14. Finding and implementing new ways to increase efficiency, commitment of employees etc..	1	2	3	4	5

Instructions for part B:

Part B presents 6 pairs of items. Look at each pair and decide which of the two is more important to you. Circle the number that applies to you, as follows:

Circle 1 if: "a" is clearly more important to you than "b" is.
Circle 2 if: "a" is somewhat more important to you than "b" is
Circle 3 if: "a" and "b" are equally important to you.

Circle 4 if: "b" is somewhat more important to you than "a" is.
Circle 5 if: "b" is clearly more important to you than "a" is.

Items	"a" Clearly more important	"a" Somewhat more important	Both Equally important	"b" Somewhat more important	"b" Clearly more important
1 a. Work demands.	1	2	3	4	5
1 b. Demands made by family members	1	2	3	4	5
2 a. Concern for job content.	1	2	3	4	5
2 b. Concern for job benefits and other advantages.	1	2	3	4	5
3 a. Concern for your own family.	1	2	3	4	5
3 b. Concern for rapid promotions	1	2	3	4	5
4 a. Job placement in your hometown or other desired place.	1	2	3	4	5
4 b. Challenging and interesting job.	1	2	3	4	5
5 a. Taking responsibility in a professional/ community service organisation.	1	2	3	4	5
5 b. Spending time with parents, relatives, or friends.	1	2	3	4	5
6 a. Continuing and concentrating on a job for a long time.	1	2	3	4	5
6 b. Searching for and obtaining job that will give better career opportunities in the future	1	2	3	4	5

Interpretation

Transfer the value of the numbers that you circled on the life orientation quiz to the blanks below. To determine percentage score, total each column. Subtract 10 from each total, then multiply by 2.5. Scores above 50 percent for either style indicate a tendency toward that style ; the higher the percentage greater the probability that that style fits you more appropriately.

Enlarging Style	Your Score	Enfolding Style	Your Score
1 a.		2 a.	
3 a.		5 a.	
4 a.		6 a.	
7 a.		8 a.	
12 a.		9 a.	
13 a.		10 a.	
14 a.		11 a.	
2 b.		1 b.	
4 b.		3 b.	
6 b.		5 b.	
Total ———			Total ———

Total Enlarging Score —————— 10 = —————— x 2.5 = ——————%
Total Enlarging Score —————— 10 = —————— x 2.5 = ——————%

■ ■ ■

Do You have the Potential to Re-invent Yourself?

We are all born with a tremendous amount of latent energy, though only a few are able to tap it says Aparna Chattopadhyay

Introspect

"A human being has so many skins covering the depths of his heart," wrote Meister Eckhart, forgetting to add that beneath these layers lies a tremendous reservoir of dormant energy waiting to be tapped. Learning this mantra to achieve success is a hard won art. Small wonder, multinational companies often sped millions on employee "re-invention," to draw the best out of their manpower resource. A common observation in organisational research is that employees often tend to indulge in unnecessary activities that deplete energy. Take this quiz to determine if you have the ability to actualise your potential. Answer each question with a 'yes' or a 'no.'

Do You Often:

1. Maintain silence, speaking only when necessary?
2. Speak in simple, easily understood language?
3. Take frequent breaks during a working day?
4. Take regular afternoon siestas?
5. Train will-power by visualising success?
6. Remain positive through all odds?
7. Look into the listener's eyes while talking?
8. Avoid straining your eyes unnecessarily?
9. Take classes in Reiki, meditation and programme yourself with auto-suggestions, such as, "just for today, I will not fear or worry"; "just for today, I will not get angry"; etc, etc.
10. Erase mental tension by becoming aware of each breath, body and your total persona?

11. Be proactive rather than waiting for circumstances to change?
12. Visualise goals before undertaking a task?
13. Prioritise work, putting first things first?
14. Think win-win most of the time?
15. Try being a good listener?
16. Practice the Gestalt school of thought believing that the whole is greater than its parts, so resources should be synergised?
17. Replenish your energy through relaxation exercise?
18. Try not to brood over problems and instead concentrate on constructive work?
19. Guard against self-condemnation?
20. Avoid hurry, scurry or being rushed-up, while trying to return to your normal calm at the earliest?

Scoring

Assign one mark for every **'yes'** answer.

Interpretation

15-20: Excellent. You know the art of tapping your potential. You fortify yourself with Emotional Intelligence and don't allow outside influences to disturb your harmony. This rewards you with mental well-being.

8-14: The difference between you and the above is the same as between a flower and a bud. You still have to blossom.

1-7: You seem to be encaged in your shell. Introspect to harness your full potential.

■ ■ ■

Your Personality – Occupational Type

All of us have to face the challenges of choosing a compatible career and finding a job that uses our talents effectively. In the process of deciding on a career, there are certain pitfalls to guard against. Most of us choose a career mostly because of the first job opportunity available. People who fall into this trap may discover later, to their regret, that they would have been happier or more successful in another line of work. Another pitfall is the choice of the job because of its external trappings, like money, prestige, power or security. In the long run, it's better to choose a work activity that is enjoyable in itself, as long as the financial rewards into it are adequate. In order to identify which type of occupation suits your personality type, take the following quiz and determine your compatible career for job satisfaction and success in life.

Following are six archetypal models of personality types. First determine the personality type which describes you most effectively. Now look for your corresponding appropriate career choice in the answers given at the end.

A. The Realistic Type: Possess good motor co-ordination and skills but lack verbal and interpersonal skills; feel somewhat uncomfortable in social settings; perceive themselves as mechanically inclined; prefer concrete to abstract problems; have conventional political and economic goals; rarely perform creatively in the arts or sciences but do like to build things with tools.

B. **The Investigative Type**: A strong scientific orientation; usually task oriented, introspective, and asocial; prefer to think through rather than act out problems; have a great need to understand the physical world; enjoy ambiguous tasks; prefer to work independently; usually perceive yourself as lacking in persuasive abilities but confident of your scholarly and intellectual abilities; have unconventional values and attitudes.

C. **The Artistic Type**: Prefer free unstructured situations with maximum opportunity for self expression; introspective and asocial but having less ego strength; greater need for individual expression; greater tendency to impulsive behaviour; creative, especially in artistic and musical media; avoid highly structured problems or physical skills; see themselves as original, intuitive, creative, non-conforming, introspective and independent.

D. **The Enterprising Type**: Possessing verbal skills suited to selling; dominating and leading; are strong leaders; have a strong drive to attain organizational goals or economic gains; tend to avoid work situations requiring long periods of intellectual effort; prefer ambiguous social tasks; a great concern for power, status and leadership; see themselves as aggressive, popular, self confident, cheerful and sociable; having high energy level.

E. **The Social Type**: Sociable, responsible; humanistic; often religious; like to work in groups; possess good verbal and interpersonal skills; avoid intellectual problem solving, physical exertion and highly ordered social activities; prefer to solve problems through feelings and interpersonal manipulation of others; enjoy activities that involve informing, curing, developing, or enlightening others; perceive themselves as understanding, idealistic and helpful.

F. **The Conventional Type**: Prefer well ordered environments; prefer systematic verbal and numerical activities; like conforming and subordinate roles; are effective at well structured tasks; avoid ambiguous situations involving interpersonal relationships or physical skills; obedient, calm, orderly and practical; identify with power and value material possessions and status.

Answer

Personality Type	Appropriate Career Choices
A.	Fish and wildlife specialist, tool designer, mechanic, engineer, electrician, and crane operator.
B.	Astronomer, biologist, chemist, technical writer, zoologist and psychologist.
C.	Artist, author, composer, writer, musician, stage director and symphony conductor.
D.	Business executive, political campaign manager, real estate sales, stock and bond sales, television producer and retail merchandising.
E.	Social worker, missionary, high school teacher, marriage counsellor, and speech therapist.
F.	Bank examiner, book keeper, clerical worker, financial analyst, quality control expert, statistician and traffic manager.

■ ■ ■

Your Work Psychology

The importance of personality factors in the employee behaviour analysis has long been recognised by researchers of Work Psychology. Personality factors have a direct bearing on the employees' work motivation, empowerment and goal achievement and tend to make or mar an individual's progress in an organisation. Organisational psychologists emphasise the role of internal (personal) factors and external (situational) factors in determining an employee's work output. The former deal with the way an employee views what happens in his organization. An employee with an "internal orientation" believes that his or her future is controlled from within. It represents self-confidence in a person's ability to control what happens to him or her in an organisation. On the contrary, an employee 'with external-others' orientation believes that his or her future is controlled by powerful others.

Yet another category of employees with an external-chance orientation believes that his or her future is controlled primarily by luck or chance. Such persons often fail to utilise their own potential in trying to achieve target goals.

Organisational research further reveals that the internal orientation of a person has a significant positive relation with his high motivation level in his work behaviour which is a prerequisite for success in organisations.

The following quiz measures an employee's orientation with respect to his internal versus external locus of control and his attitude towards work in his organisation.

Check out on "Yes" or "No" answers on the following items.
1. My success or failure depends on the amount of effort I exert.
2. The organization a person joins or the job he or she takes is an

accidental occurrence.
3. Being liked by seniors or making good impressions on them influences promotion decisions.
4. Successful completion of my assignment is due to my detailed planning and hardwork.
5. The reason I am acceptable to others in my organization is a matter of luck.
6. Preferences of seniors determine who will be rewarded in this organization.
7. Any promotion I receive in this organisation will be due to my ability and effort.
8. A person's success depends on the breaks or chances he or she receives.
9. Receiving a promotion depends on being in the right place at the right time.
10. My career depends on my seniors.
11. My success depends on my competence and hardwork.
12. Pressure groups in this organization are more powerful than individual employees are, and they control more things than individuals do.
13. The people who are important control matters in this organisation.
14. The way I work determines whether or not I receive awards.
15. If my seniors do not like me, I will not succeed in this organisation.

Scoring

Assign one mark for every **'yes'** answer. Add the total of your items separately for items in three distinct columns.

Column A		Column B		Column C	
Item No.	Score	Item No.	Score	Item No.	Score
1.		3.		2.	
4.		6.		5.	
7.		10.		8.	
11.		13.		9.	
14.		15.		12.	
Total score:		Total score:		Total score:	

Interpretation

Select the column which represents your highest total score.

A. If your score is highest for column A items, you are a person with an 'internal orientation' and believe that your future is controlled from within, denoting a high internality tendency. You have a high degree of self-confidence and have the ability to control your outside world and the environs of your organisation. You have strong convictions of self-esteem and high trust in your own abilities and are likely to make effective use of them.

B. If you sore highest on column B items, this reflects you as a person with an 'external-others' orientation and tend to believe that your future is controlled by powerful others in your organisation. A very high score indicates dysfunctional dependence on significant other people for achieving your goals. Try and change your attitude towards internality and believe more in yourself of your awareness, of your strengths and capabilities.

C. Your highest score on column C items reveals that you tend to be a person with an 'external-chance' orientation and believe that your future is controlled primarily by luck or chance. You are less likely to utilise your potential in trying to achieve goals as you believe that unforeseen factors prevent achievement of goals. An extreme view of this kind is likely to demotivate you and prove dysfunctional for utilising your potential.

To sum up, it is best to cultivate a realistic balance of external and internal orientation for effectiveness in one's organisation. Positive affirmations denoting an internal locus of control go a long way in unleashing the dormant energies from one's psychological field which are amazingly vital for organisational as well as personal success. Follow Bernard Edmond's advice as under:

To dream anything that you want to dream,
That is the beauty of human mind
To do anything that you want to do,
That is the strength of the human will.
To trust yourself to test you limits,
That is the courage to succeed.

■ ■ ■

Are You a Victim of the Achievement Trap?

Many individuals seek guidance or therapy because of the disillusionment that begins to dawn on them in their middle or later years. Their silent assumption that leads to anxiety and depression relates to their diminishing worth due to the fag end of their career. They feel threatened and long to recapture the feeling they once had from being on top. Here's the case of Rajiv.

Rajiv is a fifty-eight-year old man with a history of destructive, manic mood swings as well as incapacitating depressions. When he was a child, Rajiv's parents emphasised over and over again that his career was destined to be extraordinary, so he always felt he had to be number one. He eventually did make an exceptional contribution in his chosen field, and won numerous awards. However, as his cyclic mood disorder became increasingly severe, Rajiv began to have "high" episodes, during which his behaviour was so bizarre and disruptive that he had to be hospitalized on several occasions. Eventually, he was forced into an early retirement by the company he worked for. Twenty years of his achievement went down the drain. He became a patient of depression. However he took up re-employment again in a small company.

During the psychotherapy sessions conducted for his treatment, it was revealed that the crux of his depression was clear-cut. He was discouraged about his life because his career no longer measured up in terms of the money and prestige he had experienced in the past. While he had enjoyed the role of a charismatic young man, he was now approaching sixty and felt alone and "over the hill". Because he still believed that the only way to true happiness and personal worth was through superlative, creative achievements, he felt certain that his constricted career and modest lifestyle made him second-rate.

Like Rajiv's, there are millions of cases of victims of the Achievement Trap all over the globe. This attitude is at the core of the Western culture and the Protestant work ethic. Though it sounds innocent enough, but in fact it is self-defeating, grossly inaccurate and malignant. Rajiv's exaggerated preoccupation with his achievements is particularly common among men, who are especially vulnerable to concerns about career failure because they have been programmed from childhood to base their worth on their accomplishments. Do you also equate your worth with your achievements?

Take the following quiz and introspect a while as regards your own belief-system in this arena. Be honest and spontaneous in your answers. Do you agree or disagree with the following statements? Use the following scale for scoring your responses:

Strongly agree   : 0
Somewhat agree   : 1
Undecided   : 2
Somewhat disagree   : 3
Strongly disagree   : 4

1. "My worth as a human being is proportional to what I have achieved in my work life."
2. "After retirement I shall be unable to wield my present power and economic independence and that sure shall make me feel like a tin can that's been used and is ready for the trash".
3. "Everybody who achieves in life is particularly worthwhile just because of his or her achievement."
4. "If I have pursued a more ambitious career than my old school friend who meets me suddenly in a party, I automatically assume that my human worth is far superior to him."
5. "How can I attain self-esteem if my worth doesn't come from my success or approval?"
6. "If I give up my belief that success adds to my personal worth, then what would be the point of doing anything?"
7. "There is no *purpose* and *meaning* of life without a concept of worth."
8. "As an infant who achieves very little, an old or ill person,

or when relaxed and asleep, or just doing "nothing", one has little worth."
9. "My happiness and satisfaction depends solely on my achievements which make me feel worthy."
10. "Inspite of all my philosophizing I still feel bad about myself when I do poorly."
11. "The truly happy people are the big shots, the executives."
12. "If I'm not the greatest it means I won't get any attention from people."
13. "*Everybody* doesn't like my performance at work which proves my lack of worth."
14. "But how can *I* enjoy my work if I know I'm not the greatest?"
15. "If I were *more* famous and talented, then I'd have *more* admirers. How can I be happy on the sidelines when the big name performers with charisma are in the spotlight?"
16. "I feel that I can't get adulation and love from the opposite sex until I become a big-name talent."

Scoring

Add up all your scores on all the items.

Analysis

42 and above: You are realistic and wise enough in your approach to life. You know that the disadvantage of being a success junkie outweighs the advantages. You understand that the majority of people universally are loved and happy and well respected despite the fact that they are not "big shots" or "celebrities". Hence it *cannot* be the case that happiness and worth come only through great achievements. You are not a work-addict and like to strike a balance and synergy in life with a healthy and wholesome attitude towards it.

21-41: You tend to be fair and moderate in your interpretation of life's achievement orientation. You realize that you can not experimentally measure people's worth as well as their achievements to find out if they are in fact equal. You hold worth as worth and achievement as achievement, both being different words with different meanings.

1-20: You seem to be sadly entrapped in the Achievement Trap! You do not get the message that happiness does not reliably and necessarily follow from success, as success does not guarantee happiness. The two are not identical and are not *causally* related. So you end up chasing a mirage. Since your *thoughts* are the true key to your mood, and not success, the thrill of victory fades quickly. "The old achievements soon become old hat and you begin to feel sadly bored and empty as you stare at your trophy case," says David Burns, an eminent psychiatrist at the University of Pennsylvania.

You tend to put extra effort into your career because you're convinced this will give you extra worthiness units and therefore you see yourself as a more desirable person. You may work harder and harder to win and consequently may like yourself better. Essentially your work ethic allows you to feel you've earned personal worth and *the right* to feel happy. This belief system may make you especially motivated to produce. But have you ever looked at the other side of the coin? What are the disadvantages of your work addiction and your motto "worth equals achievement"? Don't you feel your work bug makes you so preoccupied with it that you may inadvertently cut yourself off from other potential sources of satisfaction and enjoyment as you slave away from early morning to late night? As you become more of a workaholic, you will feel excessively driven to produce because if you fail to keep up the pace, you will experience a *severe withdrawal* characterized by inner emptiness and despair. In the absence of achievement, you'll feel worthless and bored because you'll have *no other basis* for self-respect and fulfilment. Also, if your family suffers from your neglect, a certain resentment may build up. For a long time they may hold it in, but sooner or later you'll get the bill! Their coldness—leading to your lack of true self-esteem.

Introspect again, for a while—your nerves may be constantly on edge—would you still respect and love yourself if you experienced a substantial failure in your career? As with any addiction, you shall find that greater and greater doses of your "upper" will be needed in order to become "high". This tolerance phenomenon occurs with alcohol, drugs and sleeping pills. It also happens with riches, fame, and success. This is so because you automatically set your expectations higher and higher once you have achieved a particular level. The excitement quickly wears off! So get the message clear—success does not guarantee happiness. The two are not identical and are not causally related. Set up a realistic perspective towards life. Be realistic and synergistic to experience the simple joys of life as expressed by Shakespeare, "What is this life if so full of care; You have no time to stand and stare!"

■ ■ ■

Are You a Winner?

*Life's battles don't always go
To the stronger or faster man,
But sooner or later the man who wins,
Is the man who THINKS HE CAN!*

And says St. Francis of Assisi, "Start by doing what is necessary, then what is possible, and suddenly you are doing the impossible." Winning strategies such as these go a long way in the lives of achievers in different fields. A winner is often born with a positive frame of mind. A lot of research has gone into exploring the dynamics of success and failure. Histories of winners reveal that they invariably possessed certain characteristics and personality traits in common, no matter which period of history they represented. Success often leaves cues, which when followed turn into fool-proof winning strategies. Failure on the other hand is only a result of making a few mistakes repeatedly.

Are you a winner? Take the following quiz to find out.

Questions

Answer in Yes or No to the following questions. Tick mark either a or b wherever alternatives are given.

Do you mostly:

1. Start your day with a positive note by reading or listening to something positive first thing in the morning?
2. Use expressions such as "The problem is that..." when beginning your sentence?
3. Approach challenging and uphill tasks with an attitude of
   a) "It may be difficult but it is possible"
   b) "It may be possible but it is too difficult."
4. React to your mistakes at your work place as

a) "I was wrong"
   b) "It wasn't my fault"
5. Dream about your aspirations and try your best to fulfil them?
6. Choose the expression at your workplace:
   a) "That is not my job"
   b) "Let me do it for you"
7. Make yourself as part of the team in your organisation?
8. Approach a challenging job by:
   a) Seeing the gain in it?
   b) Seeing the pain in it?
9. Treat competitive situations in your organisation with an approach of :
   a) "Win/Win"
   b) "Win/ Lose"
10. Use:
    a) Hard arguments but soft words?
    b) Soft arguments but hard words?
11. a) Stand firm on your values?
    b) Compromise on your values?
12. Treat others with the philosophy:
    a) "Don't do to others what you would not want them to do to you"
    b) "Do it to others before they do it to you"
13. Plan and prepare to win; your key word being 'preparation'?
14. Make it a habit to tell yourself "let me do it now"?
15. Feel and express gratitude?
16. Follow a continuous education programme by updating yourself with the latest knowledge and technology?
17. Build a distinct positive self-esteem?
18. Stay away from negative influences?
19. Have an excuse for not doing what was needed to be done?
20. Find an answer for every problem?
21. Make a list of things you would like to change about yourself?
22. a) Seek opportunities in your work life?
    b) Seek security in your work life?

Scoring

Score one mark for every correct answer.

1, 3a, 4a, 5,6b, 7,8a, 9a, 10a, 11a, 12a, 13, 14 15, 1 6, 17, 18, 20, 21, 22a — "Yes"

2 and 19 — "No"

Interpretation

If you have scored between:

15-22: Kudos! You are well versed in the art of winning! You are a winner!

8-14: You often have a fair share of victory. Build up on it further to excel in your chosen venture.

1-7: You have yet to learn to acquire the desirable approaches for bringing effective changes in your thought and work style. Follow the advice of William James of Harvard University who said, "If you are going to change your life, you need to start immediately and do it flamboyantly." SO make conscious effort, be committed to yourself and you're sure to emerge as a winner.

■ ■ ■

Are You People-centred?

In the words of the former U.S secretary of Agriculture and a well-known religious leader Ezra Taft Benson: "Most of us consider pride to be a sin of those on top, such as the rich and the learned, looking down at the rest of us. There is, however, a far from common ailment among us – and that is pride from the bottom looking up. It is manifest in so many ways, such as fault finding, gossiping, back biting, living beyond our means, envying, coveting, withholding gratitude and praise that might lift another, and being unforgiving and jealous."

On the contrary it is the humility to realize that we are not an island, that the quality of our lives is inseparably connected to the quality of the lives of others, that meaning is not in consuming and competing, but in contributing, and the more we begin to value principles and people, the greater will be our peace, which is vital for our effective living. Effective living or being at peace with oneself is a lifetime quest. Strangely enough, the more we hanker after these virtues, the more elusive they appear. But the more we align our lives with 'giving' peace to others, the more it comes bouncing back to us. As Emerson said: "Nothing can bring you peace but yourself. Nothing can bring you peace but the triumph of principles."

Think about the following statements and check out with 'yes' or 'no' answers to these quiz items to assess your own level of people-centredness:

1. Do you restrict your security to your comfort zone alone and are somewhat chained to your plans and schedules?
2. Do you put people ahead of your schedules?
3. Are you the kind who is not into comparing, competing or

criticizing?
4. Do others begin to feel they can depend on you to be honest, direct, non-judgmental and non-manipulative, to make and keep commitments, and are quick to forgive?
5. Do you find far greater rewards in working *with* others to achieve shared vision rather than doing your own thing *to* others?
6. Are you constantly seeking to discover, understand and be continually educated by your learning and experience?
7. Do you channelise your time and energy towards contributing more than consuming, towards giving more than getting, and seeking to improve quality of life for others as well as yourself?
8. Are you careful in not burning your candle at both ends and consciously acquire new skills and ability to work with others and facilitate high-quality interdependent production?
9. Do you develop a healthy psychological immune system and can be blindsided by disease, financial set-back or disappointment and have resources to come back?
10. Do you work to create healthy immune system in your work teams, groups and organizations?
11. Do you work until you drop from exhaustion, spend until there's no credit left, or keep going on projects until you run out of time?
12. Do you focus effort during times of peak energy and creativity and take time off for recreation?
13. Do you mostly remain active physically, socially, mentally and spiritually, leading an abundant and synergistic life?
14. Does your security come from within you, from centring your lives on principles and living by your conscience, rather than from work, associations, recognition, possessions, status or any other extrinsic factor?
15. Do you radiate positive energy by seeing possibilities and neutralizing strong negative energy forces by your optimistic and positive, upbeat thought-style?
16. Do you tend to condemn yourself, your every foolish mistake or social blunder, brooding about yesterday or daydreaming

about tomorrow?
17. Is there something you feel you could always do to make a difference in the lives of people around you?
18. Do you often free yourself to work on first things first as you let go of other things and focus your time and effort on the most important ones?

Scoring

Score one mark for every correct answer.

Questions no. 2,3,4,5,6,7,8,9,10,12,13,14,15,17,18=**Yes**

Questions no. 1,11,16=**No**

Analysis

a) **Scores from 13-18**: You are a truly people-centred personality. You see life as an adventure. Your security is not in your comfort zone, but in your compass—your unique human endowments that empower you to navigate confidently in unchartered terrain. You're more synergistic. You are better able to separate the people from the problem. You are also more contribution based and lead a balanced life, not working like workaholics. There's no conscious duplicity or hypocrisy about you. You possess a fair ability to make and keep commitments to yourself and others.

b) **Scores from 7-12**: You have a fair knack to act in harmony with the principles that create peace and quality of life for you and others. You enjoy life more and cultivate a rich inner life. You focus on the things you can do something about and work to improve almost any situation you're in. You're continually educated by your experience.

c) **Scores from 1-6**: You do not seem to be at peace with yourself and people around you. The results of decades of experience in psychotherapy, positive mental attitude, and creativity development validate the futility of trying to achieve peace and long-term quality of life without the crucial element of conscience. We must become the change we seek in the world. By developing the capacity to listen to conscience and plan and organise effectively to do first things first, we can all make many individual and combined contributions that are currently falling by the wayside. We would ask you to connect deeply with your conscience for a moment and ask yourself this final question: "Is there something I feel I could do to make a difference to my work team, my organisation, my community or my society in a positive way?" And having found it, turn your resolution into reality.

■ ■ ■

Do You Work with Scientific Spirituality in Your Work Environment?

The modern man in a great hurry to acquire wealth, fame and pleasure has neither the time nor the inclination to listen to the "symphonic melody" vibrating within one's self. Thousands of systematic experiments in the field of scientific spirituality are carried out by various groups, seekers and scientists, in different parts of the world. The outcome of the preparatory stages of meditation have brought about significant changes in the work-environment and at personal level of those practising it including: a) drastic reduction in stress levels b) enhancement of personal effectiveness and c) improvement in the quality and productivity levels at work etc. Besides, with 'awareness of the moment', time management is better taken care of. In addition, the learning ability and memory power gets increased. Positive attitude towards life gets developed and interpersonal relationships become more qualitative and fulfilling. Healing of body-mind happens naturally and enhances health at all levels. In addition to all this, increased levels of patience, forgiveness, quietude, peaceful and joyous state of mind stay for longer duration. With all these, understanding of human behaviour in every situation becomes easier.

To attain all this and much more proficiency in your work-life are you making an effort to keep yourself well versed in certain spiritual dimensions? Take the following quiz and find out.

Answer the following questions by putting a tick mark against 'Mostly', 'Sometimes', 'Never'.

Do you make it a point to develop an intense and clear understanding of how your mind functions and governs your

behavioural patterns? Do you make it a point to:
1. Avoid hurrying and worrying as you go about your work? Mostly/ Sometimes/ Never.
2. Never waste a single moment of your day? Mostly/ Sometimes/ Never.
3. Never lament or regret and realize that every regret is a fresh blunder? Mostly/ Sometimes/ Never.
4. Flow with your own nature and let others flow freely in their own respective natures? Mostly/ Sometimes/ Never.
5. Have a continuous, hearty, wholesome laughter, mostly at your own self? Mostly/ Sometimes/ Never.
6. Learn both from your superiors as well as from your inferiors, from the wise as well as from the stupid? Mostly/ Sometimes/ Never.
7. Listen attentively to others with no other thought process crossing your mind? Mostly/ Sometimes/ Never.
8. Sit silently in front of a spiritual master and assimilate spiritual energy for empowering your psyche? Mostly/ Sometimes/ Never.
9. Never repress your emotions? Mostly/ Sometimes/ Never.
10. Treat humiliation gracefully by bereaving infinite pain and infinite insult without so much as raising an eyebrow? Mostly/ Sometimes/ Never.
11. Act impeccably always in every moment and according to the given situation? Mostly/ Sometimes/ Never.
12. Freely mix with others without losing your own self-confidence or uniqueness? Mostly/ Sometimes/ Never.
13. Cultivate a feeling of love and tenderness towards all cosmic beings? Mostly/ Sometimes/ Never.
14. Lose utterly your own self-importance, and immerse yourself in universal love, thus reducing yourself to zero? Mostly/ Sometimes/ Never.
15. Never indulge in judging others? Mostly/ Sometimes/ Never.
16. Find out what you most wish to do and then go and do it? Mostly/ Sometimes/ Never.
17. Know the purpose of your life and its mission and act accordingly in every moment? Mostly/ Sometimes/ Never.
18. Learn the art of ever maintaining inner silence in the midst of all the cacophony that is existing in the world? Mostly/

Sometimes/ Never.
19. Live in the society but see that the society does not live in you? Mostly/ Sometimes/ Never.
20. Be always in a state of fearlessness? Mostly/ Sometimes/ Never.
21. Immerse yourself always in the immediate task of the immediate moment? Mostly/ Sometimes/ Never.
22. Create your own reality; your belief from your experiences? Mostly/ Sometimes/ Never.
23. Realize that nothing is by chance, but everything is by choice? Mostly/ Sometimes/ Never.
24. Remind yourself that in order to live life meaningfully, and achieve your highest potential in your work, you must study spiritual science along with your formal education? Mostly/ Sometimes/ Never.
25. Remember that what you see at any given time is only a part of the truth, only one dimension of it? Mostly/ Sometimes/ Never.
26. Remember that you are rare, born here primarily for your own growth and for your own development? Mostly/ Sometimes/ Never.

Scoring

Score your answers as follows:

Mostly: 2 points
Sometimes: 1 point
Never: 0 points

Interpretation

Your level of scientific spirituality:

35-52: Excellent
18-34: Fairly good
1-17: Poor

Your Knowledge Quotient of Multi-cultural Issues

Organizations today need tools with which to explore both willingness and skills of their employees in terms of functioning effectively in a multi-cultural context. This enables them to consider other points of view from the perspective of other cultures. It also provides an insight regarding diversity issues and implicit assumptions and biases that might otherwise go unexamined. Many organizations conduct diversity training with respect to the above, without sufficient knowledge of pre-existing conditions. Diversity training, in particular can be volatile if approached incorrectly.

The following multiple-choice quiz enables you to assess yourself and your employees in this context. Encircle the correct answer to the following questions. You are not expected to know all the answers; for those answers you don't know, choose the answer that seems most likely to be correct.

1. Women who assume jobs that have been traditionally held by men often experience difficulty because
   a) They are not used to the work.
   b) Their skills have to be upgraded.
   c) They are kept on the outside by male co-workers.
   d) They are distracted by the male dominated environment.
2. Today's preferred term, used in a law and everyday life, is
   a) Physically challenged.
   b) Person with a disability.
   c) Handicapped.
   d) Crippled.
3. The "glass ceiling" theory in organizational life refers to

    a) The effect of indirect lighting on employee motivation.
    b) The high expectations, but frustrating limits that women and minorities experience in promotions.
    c) The hiring of entry level and female employees with the clear opportunity for future promotions based on performance.
    d) The feeling that many minorities and women experience being constantly watched and supervised by those above.
4. One of the most common complaints of employees with physically handicapped conditions is
    a) They are constantly taken care of by co-workers.
    b) They are treated as though they are invisible.
    c) They are asked to perform duties beyond their capabilities.
    d) They are regularly asked about their physical condition.
5. Of those taking advantage of parental leave, child-care and flex-time benefits,
    a) 90 per cent are women and 10 per cent are men.
    b) 60 per cent are women and 40 per cent are men.
    c) 75 per cent are women and 25 per cent are men.
    d) 50 per cent are women and 50 per cent are men.
6. Affirmative action programmes are designed to
    a) Give preference to female and minority candidates who may be somewhat less qualified in order to make their numbers in the work force equal to males.
    b) Open access to potential employees who have previously been excluded from equal competition for jobs within particular organizations.
    c) Fill a predetermined quota of women and minorities in an organization.
    d) Have organizations look more affirmatively on women and minorities in job evaluations than they look on males.
7. When employees have good communication skills, work teams have been shown to be more creative and productive when they are composed of people who
    a) Come from the same area of professional specialization.
    b) Have similar work and communication styles.
    c) Come from similar cultural backgrounds.

d) Come from similar educational backgrounds
   e) None of the above.
8. Among the costs that managers and their employees pay for supervising and communicating criticism and praise to female and minority employees is
   a) Limiting the employee's ability to contribute to the organisation.
   b) An increase in changes of discrimination.
   c) Support for some males who accuse the organization of unfair preferential treatment for minorities and women.
   d) Increased probability that the female or minority employee will fail.
   e) All of the above.
9. Non-verbal cues in interviews that are good indicators of a candidate's high motivation are smiling, gesturing, good eye contact, and animated verbal interchange.
   a) True
   b) False
10. One of the most frequently cited factors that women and minorities have indicated as being helpful to their advancement to top executive levels in organizations has been
    a) The need to fill a minority quota.
    b) Being seen as the best qualified candidate for the position.
    c) Having the most experience.
    d) Having been mentored and coached by significant organizational leaders.

Scoring

Question	Correct answer
1.	C
2.	B
3.	B
4.	B
5.	B
6.	B
7.	E
8.	E
9.	B
10.	D

Your score interpretation
   7 and above: Excellent
   4-6: Fairly good
   1-3: Poor

■ ■ ■

www.ingramcontent.com/pod-product-compliance
Lightning Source LLC
Chambersburg PA
CBHW070504100426
42743CB00010B/1755